TORNADO P

Ian Black

OSPREY
AEROSPACE

First published in Great Britain in 1994
by Osprey, an imprint of Reed Consumer
Books Limited
Michelin House, 81 Fulham Road,
London SW3 6RB
and Auckland, Melbourne, Singapore and
Toronto

ISBN 1 85532 429 6

Edited by Tony Holmes
Page design by Paul Kime
Printed and bound in Hong Kong
Produced by Mandarin Offset

Front cover The distinctively marked
75th anniversary Tornado F.3 of No
25(F) Sqn streams wingtip vortices in the
moist air off the coast of Gibraltar as the
pilot, Flt Lt Archie Neill, practices his 67°
full-sweep airshow manoeuvre for the
benefit of the author's camera

Back cover Sweltering in the midday
heat on the baking Akrotiri flightline,
air- and groundcrew closely monitor the
twin Turbo-Union RB.199 engines of a
No XI Sqn F.3 as they spool up at the
start of another gunnery sortie during
the unit's Armament Practice Camp
(APC) in 1992

Title page Navigator Flt Lt Jim Brown
glances up from the back seat of his
Tornado F.3 as Flt Lt Archie Neill flies
the specially marked No 25(F) Sqn
display jet beneath my aircraft. Passing
barely 50 ft below us, the F.3 was
photographed four miles off the coast of
Gibraltar as the crew practised their
display prior to the colony's Air Day in
September 1991. To achieve this
distinctive planform shot we started off
in close formation and banked into a left-
hand turn. At a pre-arranged time,
Archie flew underneath me, moving
from one side to the other and thus
allowing me to take an impressive top
view of the jet – the close proximity of
the F.3 is illustrated by the fact that I
shot this photograph with a standard 50
mm lens mounted to my Nikon. I flew
the back-up jet for the display crew to
Gibraltar, a job I performed on two or
three occasions during the 1991 season.
The whole squadron takes it in turns to
fill this weekend tasking.

Flt Lts Neill and Brown earned the
right to display the F.3 in 1991 after a fly-
off that involved all three Leeming-
based Tornado squadrons. A good
combat pilot doesn't always make a
successful display pilot. The latter has to
know both how to best exploit his jet
aerobatically, and be enthusiastic and
positive about his aircraft, and the RAF
in general, when on the ground. Each
potential display pilot has his own
'secret' routine which he flies for the
approval of the station commander, who
gets to experience these at first-hand
during a back-seat check flight early on
in the pre-season work-ups.

Once the pilot and squadron have
been chosen for the coming season, an
aircraft is often allocated as the airshow
mount and marked up in a one-off
scheme designed by the unit and
approved by the station commander –
the No 25(F) Sqn jet wore a scheme
devised by Sqn Ldr Ian Howe, who was
ably assisted by Archie Neill. The F.3
was resprayed with special paint that
adhered to the airframe at speeds in
excess of 700 mph

For a catalogue of all books published by Osprey Aerospace
please write to:

**The Marketing Department, Reed Consumer Books,
1st Floor, Michelin House, 81 Fulham Road, London SW3 6RB**

Above Eager to close the canopy and shut out the cold January air at Leeming, a pair of Canadian Armed Forces (CAF) pilots complete their preflight checks against the backdrop of a weak winter sun. The Baden-Söllingen-based CF-18s were occasional visitors to Leeming up until their return to Canada in 1992/93, handfuls of Hornets flying from the station during weapons or ECM dets to the Spadeadam ranges in Cumbria. This CF-18B had been despatched to the UK by No 439 'Tiger' Sqn in January 1992 in preparation for a large deployment to Lossiemouth the following month for a naval exercise north west of the Shetlands. You had to admire the professionalism and commitment of these pilots flying CAP missions in a single-seat jet over the freezing North Sea, 150 miles from Lossiemouth in the middle of February – a long way away from Canada! The job of protecting the 'friendly' vessels was shared with Leeming-based F.3 units, hence the CF-18B visit

Introduction

The question I'm most frequently asked is 'what made you start taking photographs?' My passion for photography began at school, where I learnt the art of black and white developing using basic equipment in less than ideal conditions. Having joined the RAF in 1978, I spent my first operational tour flying in the back seat of Phantom FGR.2s over Germany.

I wanted to capture the images I saw so that those less fortunate than myself – ground-based mortals – could see what it's really like to spend your life flashing around at high speed low to the ground. To capture the sensation of flight actually on film isn't easy, and side views of aircraft at medium altitude say nothing. One has to incorporate movement, light and atmosphere into each shot. It isn't enough to simply point and shoot. A good photograph is all about lighting. You have to make the best of what is available from dawn to dusk, rain or shine.

In fifteen-plus years of flying I've been airborne at every hour in the day, trying to capture the mood in each situation. The art of successful aviation photography is a combination of attempting to capture ten tons of airborne metal in an instant, showing in a solitary image speed, power and G forces – in short, the secret of 'flight'.

Where possible I use a standard 50 mm F1.4 lens for air-to-air photography as this provides the best distortion free image when shooting through thick perspex or armour-plated glass. Zoom lenses are rarely used due to their inferior optical quality – wide-angles are employed occasionally, but their use necessitates flying in uncomfortably close formation with your subject! Due to the make up of the canopy perspex, lenses above 80 mm don't really work. The same applies for UV and polarizing filters.

I've used a variety of cameras over the years and my favourite for air-to-air work is the old Canon T90, which was basically the last word in manual camera design. Now I have a Nikon F4 and a Canon EOS 5. The Nikon is a straight no nonsense workhorse whereas the Canon is unbelievably light and packed full of innovative ideas. The quality of the optics in this camera are also quite astounding. The film I shoot with is predominantly Fuji Velvia because of its saturated colours, which are ideal for air-to-air photography.

I hope the photographs in this volume do justice to the fast jet aircrew of the RAF, because without their help and co-operation this book would never have been done. My thanks are also extended to the pilots of other nations who have helped in the production of this book, as well as editor Tony Holmes for his work on the manuscript, and his technical knowledge. Finally, a big thank you to my wife Jane and my children Timothy and Hannah

Right Lightning F.6 XS904 was photographed over the North Sea with British Aerospace test pilot Peter Gordon-Johnson at the controls, the jet being flown back to Warton after its participation in the last No 19(F) Sqn reunion to be held at Wildenrath in October 1991. This occasion also signalled the final visit to Germany by a Lightning, and the jet was suitably 'zapped' with a blue rendition of the squadron's dolphin badge on its markingless tail. It almost brought tears to my eyes to be flying in such close proximity to a Lightning again, having not sat in one for over three years. I had flown this jet out of Warton in February 1988 as the aircraft was being cleared to operate with overwing tanks once again, prior to the radar trials work commencing

Contents

Black autobiography

Right My first taste of frontline flying came with No 19(F) Sqn at Wildenrath following the successful completion of my navigation course. A posting to RAF Germany on Phantom FGR.2s was considered by many in the know to offer the best possible fast jet flying available to navigators in the RAF, Nos 19(F) and 92 Sqns fulfilling their vital NATO air defence tasking at mission heights of 250 ft! Cruising along at a somewhat greater height than what was considered to be the norm for Wildenrath FGR.2s purely for photographic purposes, this grimy jet was being flown on this occasion by the then station commander, Gp Capt (now Air Vice Marshal) John Allison. The last Phantom II in Germany to be fitted with the rectangular fin tip radar warning receiver (RWR) housing, this jet was, conversely, one of the first FGR.2s resprayed in air defence grey – so early, in fact, that it was painted in a trial matt shade, which proved too susceptible to scuffing and absorption of flightline dirt. Other FGR.2s were resprayed with greys that exhibited a modicum of lustre, and therefore a resistance to scuffing, as a result of RAFG's experience with this jet.

The Phantom IIs were almost always flown armed with the centre-line gun due to the very real threat of the Cold War in the early 1980s. We were constantly preparing for action, and when the alert siren signalled a practice scramble, you often thought that perhaps this time it was for real. The threat in those days was the *Fishbed* and *Flogger Bravo*, whilst things like the MiG-29 and Su-27 were still only fuzzy pictures – just as well really as both types would have been a hard match for the FGR.2. Technology has marched on appreciably in the decade since I was in Germany, and even during the four years that I was there, we progressed from fly CAPs with Dutch and Belgian F-104s in 1981, to performing similar sorties with F-16s from the same countries, plus USAFE F-15s, by 1984. Our AWG-12B airborne missile control system, which combined the Westinghouse APQ-59 pulse-Doppler radar with the ASW-25 weapon control computer, was very good, and easily on a par with the F-16A's Westinghouse APG-66 system, plus the two-man crew in our Phantom IIs helped in co-ordinating CAPs.

The SUU-23/A gun pod, which housed an M61 Vulcan cannon, was a familiar store in Germany, despite the fact that its effectiveness as an air-to-air weapon was marginal when compared with modern gun systems. The scores achieved on APCs were never brilliant, the average being about 15 to 20 per cent on a towed banner. By comparison, the F-16 and the Tornado F.3 have their gun linked to the radar and HUD, thus allowing an average shot to score 40 to 50 per cent and a marksman anything up to 100 per cent. The size and weight of the SUU-23/A also caused headaches, as being strapped to the underside of the aircraft, any heavy landing would move the gun slightly and thus de-harmonise it! In a war situation you would have to resort to pressing the trigger and walking the bullets onto the target

Above The FGR.2 was ideal for the job in Germany as it was fast at low-level, possessed an excellent radar, could carry a lot of weapons and had a two-man crew. In its day it was the best in its class. All our flying was done at 250 ft AGL (Above Ground Level), including transits to and from our patrol areas. We never went above 1000 ft, unless the weather was very bad or we were performing a night or combat sortie. The radar worked extremely well at this height, the AWG-12 picking up targets over land at distances in excess of 30 miles away. Although solidly built, the airframe was G-limited in some configurations, and towards the end of my tour the big drawback with the jet was that it couldn't turn with either an F-15 or an F-16. By comparison, in the days of the F-104 it really held its head up. This atmospheric shot was taken at Gutersloh in November 1981 moments after XV496 had arrived for a forward deployment to 'Battle Flight', which was housed in the station's old Lightning sheds. The squadron would despatch a pair of jets to Gutersloh and maintain readiness on the border for a 24- or 48-hour period. The aircraft would be 'cocked' on a five-minute readiness state,

and once scrambled you were only two or three minutes flying time away from the then East German border. Patrolling in this area was quite exciting as you would fly up to the 'Wall' and look over, making sure that you didn't accidentally stray into Communist airspace

Above right It was very unusual to see an FGR.2 airborne without the mandatory 270 US gal Sgt Fletcher external tanks, SUU-23/A gun pod and Sidewinder rails. In fact, about the only time this occurred was during a combat work-up phase, and to aid in the realism of the training, XV480's solitary store is a finless AIM-9G acquisition round. The hazy backdrop to this photograph is typical of the weather encountered in the region during the warmer months of the year. Low-level navigation is very difficult in Germany because all the country towns are similar in appearance – they are all basically big circular villages with a cathedral or church, that invariably boasts a spire, in the centre. Therefore, at 420 kts with 250 ft AGL on the altimeter, everywhere looks the same! There were TACAN (Tactical Air

Navigation) networks around, but they only covered 20-mile areas when you were flying at low-level. You had to maintain a constant vigil to ensure that you didn't stray over the built up areas of Bonn, Dusseldorf or Cologne. During my time in Germany all the aeroplanes were eventually resprayed in air defence grey, and the effectiveness of the new scheme varied primarily on the weather conditions. On a hazy day like this one the jet would disappear, whereas the grey/green FGR.2 would stand out. Conversely, sometimes it was good to remain visible, particularly if you were flying along in battle formation (line abreast with two miles separation) as it could be extremely tiring if were constantly losing sight of your wingman.

My tour at Wildenrath coincided with the end of an era which had commenced in the 1950s and dragged on into the early 1980s. In the past you could patrol around over Germany and 'hassle' with any other NATO aircraft unbriefed, as well as fly in any weather. Most of our jets were ex-RAFG strike Phantom IIs that had been passed on to Nos 19(F) and 92 Sqns following the arrival of Jaguar GR.1s at Brüggen in 1975/76. Initially delivered

to No 31 Sqn in 1971, this particular FGR.2 was finally scrapped at Wattisham in September 1991 following its retirement from No 56 Sqn.

Due to the high perceived threat during the early 1980s we had to always have six or seven jets out of ten fully operational at the beginning of every day. If this meant that groundcrews had to work throughout the night to achieve this then so be it. Our engineering section was very dedicated at Wildenrath, and the squadron never fell short on airframes during my tour in Germany.

Flying air defence with RAFG was considered to be the best possible tour within the community, and we all viewed ourselves as the 'creme de la creme' of the air force's fighter crews! We thought that we were far better than the UK Air defence guys, although many RAFG crews returning to units at Leuchars and Wattisham had trouble adjusting to patrol heights that covered the range from sea level to 50,000 ft. In Germany we had the straightforward task of tackling targets in the low-level band from 250 to 1000 ft, in all weathers

Above In February 1989 I left Phantom IIs for Chipmunk T.10s as I began my conversion from the back to the front seat. Having joined the RAF from the Army five years earlier on an eight-year short service commission, I requested a transfer to be a pilot on a permanent commission, and my bid was duly accepted. I had originally been streamed onto the navigation course back in 1979 because at the time I showed a better aptitude for back-seat rather than front-seat flying – there was also a surplus of pilots at the time. I successfully completed the 15-hour course on Chipmunks at the Flying Selection Squadron (FSS) at RAF Swinderby and then faced a four-month hold prior to commencing my training at No 7 FTS at Church Fenton. Having had a taste of Chipmunks I decided to gain a little more experience on the 'tail dragger', so I held at No 6 Air Experience Flight (AEF), which was then at Abingdon but has since moved to Benson.

The chances of scrounging air time here were far greater than with a Tornado or Jaguar unit. During my three-month stay I learnt to respect the diminutive Chipmunk, which proved to be a difficult aircraft to fly well! Compared to a jet fighter, in which

things tend to happen quite quickly, in a Chipmunk strong gusts of wind as you are coming in to land can put you out of control equally as quick. You have got to be on top of things at all times, and practice good hand and eye co-ordination. On one occasion I was flying with the pilot of this aircraft, Sqn Ldr Mike Neill, and we landed into a 40-kt headwind. Due to my lack of experience, we bounced back up to a height of about 15 ft on touchdown with a forward speed of 50 kts, so by the time the headwind had been taken into account, we were basically hovering for a few seconds, with my forward speed at no more than 3 mph! I then attempted to pull off one of the few vertical/rolling landings ever performed in a Chipmunk, much to Mike Neill's amusement

Above right The Jet Provost T.3A at No 7 FTS provided me with my first real taste of fast jet 'piloting', although my failure to be startled by its rather tame performance on my first incentive ride did put my instructor's nose slightly out of joint! As it trundled down the runway at 90 kts following our last landing the ex-Buccaneer pilot asked me for my first impressions, and I said it

felt like flying in a helicopter(!), seeing as I had just finished an 800-hr tour on Phantom FGR.2s! That said, it was not an easy aircraft to fly, being very heavy on the controls. The side-by-side seating also took some getting used to as the instructor would be watching your every move and there was no way you could bluff your way through, particularly when it came to navigation. Learning to plot and fly a course at high altitude using a map, kneeboard and a pencil, without autopilot, was a nerve racking experience, particularly when you didn't trust your instructor's advice about a correctly trimmed jet flying itself – after about three years and 1000 hours of stick time you realise they were right all along!

I spent just over seven months on the T.3A, accumulating 60 hours in my log book. Your progress was assessed every 10 to 15 hours through general handling or instrument flying tests, and major mid and end of course checks were also performed. Everyone said that I would find the conversion easier due to my frontline tour, but I don't think that was the case at all. Admittedly, I didn't find the claustrophobic and restrained environment of the cockpit alien in any way, but the increased

workload of the pilots' course compared to my previous experience with the navigators' syllabus was a bit of a shock. During the latter you only flew once a week, and spent the remainder of your time in the simulator. With pilot training you often fly twice a day and you could go very quickly from being quite good to having a couple of bad trips, and before you know it the instructors are saying 'you could be reaching a capacity problem', and once on the slippery slope it's hard to claw your way back. The pilots' course is three years long and it's like having someone watching you every day throughout that time – it takes total dedication to succeed. Fortunately, I did well enough to be selected for Group One, which is fast jets, and progressed on to the Jet Provost T.5A, which felt like an F-16 when compared to the T.3A! In reality the only differences were a pressurized cockpit and no tip tanks, the deletion of the latter increasing its top end speed by all of five knots or so!

Regressing to the T.3A for a moment, this formation shot was taken in March 1985 from an open cockpit Jet Provost, the pilot instructing me to wind the canopy back so that I could take a clearer picture of the trio of No 7 FTS machines!

Right With roughly 100 hours on Jet Provosts I moved to north Wales and RAF Valley in August 1985, where I joined No 4 FTS. There I basically flew the Jet Provost course once again, but 100 kts faster. The tandem seat layout and the near supersonic capabilities of the Hawk T.1 provide the would-be pilot with a taste of what lays in store for him should he graduate successfully. Following a series of dual check rides and the completion of circuit work, you are unleashed on a brief solo flight. The traditional thing to do on this 20-minute sortie is fly once around the island of Anglesey as fast as you dare and then recover back at Valley to execute your first solo landing – always a tense affair. Instrument flying, high-level max-rate turns and basic aerobatics fill the next few months, your body slowly becoming acclimatised to pulling high-G manoeuvres over a sustained period. A mid-course handling check ensures that your progress is up to scratch, and then the final few months are spent criss-crossing Wales and the rest of England and Scotland on low-level navigation sorties as a prelude to the Tactical Weapons Unit (TWU) training.

One of the Hawk's great advantages over the Jet Provost, and the two-seat Hunter that it replaced at Valley, was that you had the ability to fly virtually anywhere in the UK at high level, let down for the low-level navigation portion of the sortie, go back to high-level upon the completion of your tasking, and return to base still with enough fuel to divert if the weather had clagged in in Wales. This particular photograph features Flt Lts Paul Warren and Simon 'Shifty' Young formating with myself and Lt Masson, a French exchange instructor, during a flyby over Shawbury. The sortie lasted an hour and 15 minutes and I had 'sandbagged' the flight simply by ringing up one of the squadrons and enquiring whether any instructors were scheduled for solo sorties. Valley was always good for 'passenger flying', and during the six months I was there I managed to fly an extra 20 hours. You could help your pilot out during the flight by reading off the frequencies and generally keeping a sharp lookout for other aircraft. The term 'sandbagging' has its origins in the days of the Royal Flying Corps when to keep the weight of a two-seat aircraft correct on a solo flight a sandbag was placed in the spare seat as ballast. Only instructors could fly with students in the back as we did not yet have our wings, and it was deemed that two students together would have far too much fun!

In April 1986 I moved on to RAF Brawdy and No 1 Tactical Weapons Unit, equipped with Hawk T.1As. Following one more check ride we were thrust headlong into the fighter course learning all the things that comprise the day-to-day flying on a frontline squadron – a mix and match of air-to-air gunnery, low-level navigation, air combat, bombing and strafing, and formation flying, including tactical turns and learning to fly in battle formation, firstly at medium altitude and then at low-level. Upon the successful completion of his TWU course, the fledgling aviator is at last recognised as a pilot within the RAF by his peers. After three long years I was finally posted to my dream tour in September 1986 – Lightnings at RAF Binbrook

Left I had watched my father fly Lightnings as a little boy and it was an aeroplane that had always stirred my heart for many reasons – its British design, its 1950s attributes, its flying quality and its charisma. Each aeroplane looked different to me, as opposed to today's F-16s, for example, which all look the same. My fascination for Lightnings could be equated with a steam buff's love of locomotives – the aircraft, like a hissing train, exuded life. A big and strong jet, I was massively impressed by the amount of thrust available from its twin Rolls-Royce Avon engines even as late as 1986. It must have felt incredible to pilots back in 1960, having come from Hunters or Meteors. It was just like sitting on two 'aluminium rocket tubes', as you only had to push the throttle forward by a few inches and you rocketed from 150 to 600 kts in a matter of seconds. You strapped the Lightning on to your back, rather than climb into it like a modern fighter, and the sights and smells that greeted you upon arrival were like those associated with walking into an antiques shop – lots of hand-fashioned dials and instruments and the all pervading smell of leather. It was beautifully British! Ergonomically, the cockpit was superbly laid out, and the Ferranti AI-23B Airpass fire-control radar system was incredibly effective even at this late stage in the aircraft's distinguished career.

The pilot of this fighter was none other than Gp Capt (now Commodore) John Spencer, the last station commander at Binbrook. This was his own aircraft, and it was quite an old F.6, having originally been delivered to No 23 Sqn as an F.3 on 17 March 1965. It was latterly used by the Lightning Training Flight (LTF) as a target aeroplane, hence the fact it wore the Binbrook station crest on the tail – it was also unusual because its designated pilot was a Group Captain, and it therefore wore his rank pennant beneath the cockpit and his initials on the fin. The jet always flew with Firestreak missiles fitted as Gp Capt Spencer believed (quite rightly so, due to his huge experience on the Lightning) that the missiles' fins acted as miniature canards, thus allowing you to get more lift off the front of the aircraft in combat, and giving you better nose authority in general.

We had just completed a general handling sortie and were commencing a Ground Controlled Approach (GCA) over Grimsby into Binbrook through the thick cloud bank below when this photo was taken from a No XI Sqn T.5, capably flown on this occasion by Flt Lt Steve 'Shunty' Hunt. GCA landings in close formation are hard work, and if you're lucky you'll put the gear and flaps down in the daylight prior to plunging into the mist. Sometimes you would fly so close in cloud that all you would see of your number two were his wingtip lights, the rest of his jet disappearing in the 'clag'. If you lose sight of the aircraft for longer than a second you have to pull out of formation and follow the set 'lost leader in cloud' procedure, which sees you level off and make contact once again using the R/T. Separate approaches to the runway are then made.

The Lightning was not speed stable on approach, and one had to constantly move the throttle to maintain the correct speed. It wasn't an easy jet to land for a novice pilot like myself, but you had bags of power in reserve should you happen to get low on the glideslope

Right This LTF F.3 carries a pair of finless Red Top acquisition rounds, the Binbrook armourers fitting the heat-seeking missiles to the aircraft devoid of their flying surfaces as they had a tendency to break off at high speed! By the time this photograph was taken in 1987, the Hawker Siddeley Dynamics missile was at least a decade past its sell by date, its launch profiles being limited to a 30° tail attack on a target – its performance was equitable with the Bravo model AIM-9. Having said that, a lot of the live firings performed by Nos 5 and XI Sqns in the time I was on Lightnings were very successful, which said something for the build quality of the Firestreak and Red Top as many of the rounds fired had sat in packing crates for 20 years or more. By the time the Lightnings were finally phased out in mid-1988 we had actually run out of targets at which to fire missiles, leaving dozens of rounds to be destroyed in their crates, and fortunately never used in anger.

You had to work harder in a Lightning to achieve a missile shot than in a Tornado F.3 as in the former you had to do everything yourself. This applies particularly to an out of parameters shot, as you may be head out of the cockpit keeping a visual on the target and just as you are about to loose off a missile your navigator will tell you that you're out of the weapon's lock-on parameters. In the Lightning a similar scenario would have resulted in a wasted shot. The most demanding intercepts that we flew with the Lightning were called 'Saturns', and they were only flown by fully qualified combat pilots. The sortie commenced at a flexible CAP height and GCI would then vector you onto an unknown contact which could be flying at any altitude between 250 and 70,000 ft. The aim of course was to intercept the target, and all your skills were tested during the mission. The sortie could see you chasing a low-level threat, which was handled in a certain way, or a high flyer copying a U-2 or *Foxbat* profile, or maybe a medium bomber attack, a defector or perhaps a long-range fighter. The list was long, and I remember all the profiles very well!

Everything you did in the Lightning had to be worked out in your head, so all your turning keys for intercepts were thought out mentally. For example, if you had a target flying above 30,000 ft you would pick him up on the radar and commence a set of procedures to intercept the threat which had been learnt earlier, parrot fashion. Similarly, a low-level target would be handled in the same way – for every attack profile there was a set procedure to intercept the target. Therefore, as soon as the threat was picked up on radar you had five or six seconds to work out its height, heading and speed, plus choose your attack profile and how you would go about intercepting it, whilst constantly worrying about your fuel state. There was no point in going off and successfully attacking a supersonic target at 70,000 ft only to find yourself 200 miles away from Binbrook with barely enough Avtur to get you to the nearest oil rig.

Fuel was a constant problem, and on the LTF, as part of your training, they would try and run you dry, not to be awkward, but to teach you the hard way that there were no reserves of Avtur in the Lightning. After a while you developed a situational awareness second to none, whereby you could be doing an intercept at the same time as your brain was creating a map in your mind of where both you and the fuel were going. To help feed the mental calculations you periodically swept the coastline with the radar, scanned your fuel gauges diligently and watched the TACAN. The Lightning could tackle any threat at all altitudes, but its radar was optimised for medium level targets over the sea – overland threats had to be acquired visually

Left and above Just how I got three Lightnings together in the same patch of sky four years after the jets had been retired from RAF service is quite a complicated story! The F.6s had been flying as targets for British Aerospace over the Aberporth range in Cardigan Bay, Wales, since mid-1988, and No XI Sqn had been involved with the Warton-based jets throughout 1992. The completion of the Foxhunter trials later that same year signalled the end of the Lightning fleet's useful life with British Aerospace. With little time left to shoot these aircraft in their natural environment, I quickly organised a sortie for 16 December 1992; this was in fact the last time that all three jets flew together before retirement. The trials flying manager actually phoned me up and asked me if I could provide a jet from which to photograph this historic formation but unfortunately the squadron was already fully committed. However, CFS at Valley offered up a Hawk, piloted by another ex-Lightning pilot! As a trade off for providing the jet, one of the Lightnings was scheduled to do a practice diversion to Valley during the flight as a 'thank you' from Warton.

The weather was shocking in all directions, bar a patch of clear sky 50 miles west of Warton, so after a full briefing from the met man at Valley we arranged to rendezvous with the three-ship here. I briefed the pilots to fly a simple formation as it's easier to get the shots you want from one straight forward angle, than 20 complex manoeuvres that could take all your air-to-air time up just in the positioning of the jets. I always try and spend as little time as possible taking the photographs as that is always the secondary aim of the mission.

The F.6 closest to the camera, flown here by the legendary Keith Hartley, was the last Lightning sent to Warton for the trials flight, arriving in Lancashire on 11 July 1989. Initially delivered to the RAF in late 1966, XR773 flew with Nos 74 and 56 Sqns before finding its way to Binbrook and No 5 Sqn, after which it spent the rest of its service life shuffling between the two surviving Lightning squadrons until the jet's final retirement from active service in June 1988. It was initially stored at the Aircraft & Armaments Experimental Establishment (A&AEE) at Boscombe Down prior to being issued to Warton. Despite having spent over a year in a hangar in Wiltshire, the aircraft's systems and radar functioned fine when the time came for it to head north

Above Prior to the formation joining up we rendezvoused with XP693, which was being capably flown by Peter Orme, on its way to Valley, and this gave me the opportunity to work over the jet at close quarters, with the bleak Welsh coastline as a suitable backdrop. The oldest Lightning in the flight, this jet was in fact the first production F.3 built by English Electric at Warton, flying on 16 June 1962. As such, it was never actually issued to a frontline unit, the airframe spending all of its RAF career at the A&AEE and the Royal Aircraft Establishment (RAE), where it was used for F.6 trials work. Fully updated to the ultimate Lightning spec, XP693 eventually found its way back to British Aerospace in 1977, where it was gainfully employed as a chase plane for the Tornado F.2/3 and latterly as a target aircraft.

Boasting far fewer flying hours than its frontline contemporaries, the aircraft was fitted with a Ferranti FIN 1064 digital navigation and attack system, as carried in the Jaguar GR.1, for the Foxhunter radar trials. Normallyy, the F.6s flew with the distinctive 270-gal overwing subsonic tanks permanently attached, further increasing the Lightning's limited endurance by about 20 minutes – a refuelling probe was also a standard fit, the fleet utilizing Warton-based Buccaneer S.2A XN974 for aerial tanking

Right My last Lightning flight took place in June 1988, and almost immediately I left the elite single-seat day fighter world and returned to the massed ranks of the two-seat air defence community, joining No 229 Operational Conversion Unit's ground school for the Tornado F.3 at Coningsby. Over the next five months I learnt to fly and fight the new interceptor, firstly in the simulator and then for real with an instructor in the back seat. My first impression of the jet was just how complex a weapon system it was, the crew being literally bombarded with information when it came to target prosecution. By contrast, the Lightning's radar provided you with little more than a blip on the screen, the height, speed and intercept profile to be flown against the threat being figured out through mental gymnastics in your head. With the F.3, you can acquire and track multiple targets, with the relevant information for each contact being quickly flashed up on the Head-Down Display (HDD). Moreover, details from the navigator's Tactical Evaluation Display can be automatically displayed on my head-down screen. Radar Warning Receivers (RWRs) alerting you to further threats were also a revelation – RWRs never quite made it to Binbrook! The added firepower of six extra (modern) missiles was also most welcome.

Ergonomically speaking, the F.3's cockpit was much larger than the Lightning, and the Martin-Baker Mk10 seat was far more comfortable than their Mk2 device, as fitted in the F.6. The heavier G-suit and new technology helmet took some getting used to, however, as did the two sets of leg restraints. On the flying side of things, the wing-sweep seemed very unusual at first, the idea of having to fly and fight the jet, and alter the wings at the same time, being difficult to grasp initially. However, after 200 to 300 hours in the jet it became second nature. The F.2/3 was always scheduled to have an auto-sweep from Day One, but as the crews soon became familiar with the variable-geometry wing, it was deemed an unecessary 'luxury'. I enjoyed my five months on the OCU, and the course structure itself gave me an excellent insight into the Tornado's potential. Only five former No XI Sqn pilots transitioned from Lightnings to Tornados, the remaining eight being either too senior for the conversion or retiring from the air force altogether. I left Coningsby with 70 hours on the F.3 in my logbook, having flown air combat; affiliation against low-level targets; worked as constituted two- or four-ship packages on air-to-air sweeps; day flight refuelling; and night flying. Today's F.3 is a far cry in terms of its capability from the jets I flew at the OCU in 1988, improvements brought in during and after the Gulf War having changed the aircraft in many respects

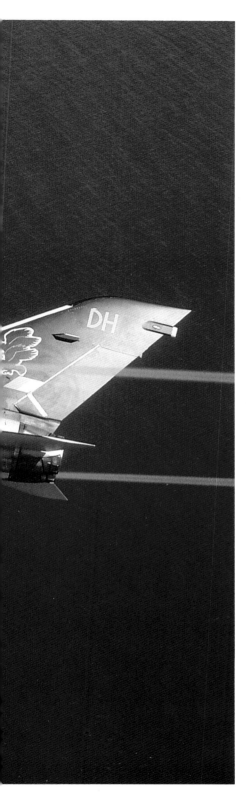

RAF Leeming

Left Although my first frontline posting on the F.3 was to No 23 Sqn, I regularly photographed aircraft of all three Leeming-based units during my four-year stay at the North Yorkshire station. This beautifully marked jet was captured on film during a special sortie organised by No XI Sqn for the BBC *Look North* programme, the flight coinciding with my former unit's first anniversary as a Tornado squadron, celebrated on 1 July 1989. This distinctive jet belonged to the unit's first F.3 boss, Wg Cdr David Hamilton, and as No XI Sqn's two-letter tailcode range covered DA to DZ, it seemed only appropriate for him to adopt DH. ZE764 was actually the first F.3 issued to the unit, having arrived at Coningsby on 25 April 1988 whilst the 'new' No XI Sqn was still only a 'Designate' outfit – this obviously changed on 1 July when the last Lightning landed at Cranfield. The all-black fin on the aircraft was a carry over from the old F.6 days as the squadron commander's jet at Binbrook also boasted a similar solid coloured spine and vertical surface. No XI Sqn was also the first F.3 unit not to modify its emblem into an arrowhead, preferring to keep its traditional twin eagles motif unchanged on the tail and only carry fighter bars on either side of the roundel.

Like the rest of the squadron's baseline F.3s, ZE764 was swapped for a newly delivered Stage One modified aircraft as issued to the Leuchars Wing during the *Operation Granby* switch around in August 1990. Whilst in Scotland its black fin was removed, and although the jet returned to the No XI Sqn fold as DH soon after the unit returned to Leeming in December 1990, the new officer commanding decided not to restore the aircraft to its former glory.

The crew for this photo flight consisted of Sqn Ldr Paul Burnside up front and Flt Lt 'Ginge' Richards in the back. Paul, a Qualified Flying Instructor and now with Cathay Pacific, was the first pilot in the RAF to pass the 1000-hour mark on F.2/3s, whilst 'Ginge', a Qualified Weapons Instructor, later became my navigator when I joined No XI Sqn. The rarity of this photograph cannot be overstated as F.3s are seldom flown out of Leeming toting a full missile fit and 2250 l external tanks – the spotless finish of the ordnance mirrors that of the aircraft itself

Above and left Proving that Leeming pilots can hold a tight formation just as well as the Red Arrows, this impressive Diamond Nine was put up for a Royal flypast in July 1991. The formation was made up of three jets from each of the station's squadrons, and I had clearance to tag along in the spare F.3 and record this historic event on film. The tenth aircraft is known as the 'whip' and its pilot feeds the remaining nine crews correct heading vectors, thus allowing them to accurately formate as briefed on the ground. However, as is often the case, what actually transpired once airborne deviated somewhat from the plan and the 'whip' aeroplane was forced to fill a gap left by a jet that went unserviceable on start up. I was occupying the back seat in the spare, and my pilot had to take up one of the central positions in the formation, which I wasn't overly pleased about at the time! As it happens, this turn of events allowed me to take some very unusual shots which graphically illustrate just how close formating jets get in the Diamond Nine.

An hour's flying in one of these formations requires some serious concentration on the part of the crew, and the flight briefing usually takes far longer than any other peacetime sortie as everybody must know where to go in the event of an emergency. For example, if you're in the middle of the formation and you have an engine fire, the last thing you want to do is pull up or move to the right – you just can't do it! Everyone, therefore, has their own briefed escape routes to take in case of an incident.

Formation reference points like a squared off jet pipe and the anti-collision lights on the fin are used for accurate station keeping. Usually, the pilot will line up his aircraft with others in the formation by using two reference points – the lights on the wingtip and fin, for example. When they are all in line, you know that you are in the correct spot within the Diamond Nine. Navigators also play a vital role by keeping a good general lookout, a function which is near impossible for the pilot to perform whilst holding position with the other eight aircraft

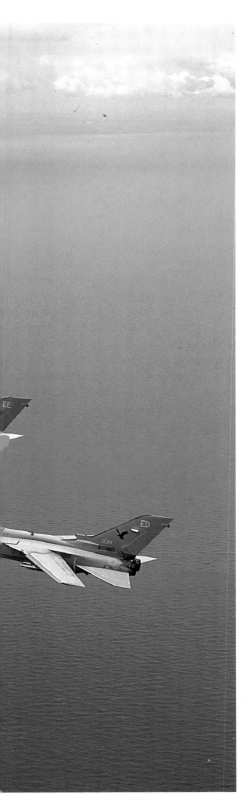

Left This is what a Diamond Nine formation looks like from the 'whip' jet, rather than from the middle slot! Princess Margaret visited Leeming on 25 June 1991 to congratulate the squadrons on their work in the Gulf, and to honour her visit three jets from each unit were freshly adorned with full markings and put aloft – this was the first post-Gulf application of squadron colours at the station, and a close look at the tails of all nine jets reveals that the air defence grey immediately surrounding each badge differs from that which adorns the rest of the airframe. The sortie was led by Sqn Ldr Ian Howe from No 25(F) Sqn, and the physical arrangement of the F.3s within the formation was done so as to symmetrically group the aircraft by unit. The planning, briefing and physical leading of the Diamond Nine is always entrusted to a flight or squadron commander who has been part of a similar formation at least once before

Above Following the successful completion of *Operation Granby*, the composite squadron of F.3s at Dhahran began returning to the UK from 13 March 1991 onwards. All 18 aircraft flown by the unit had been fully upgraded to Stage One specs prior to being despatched to Saudi Arabia the previous August. Further aircraft received the upgrades (see chapter three for full details) whilst the war raged in the Middle East, and by the time the F.3s returned to the UK, a decision had been made to equip all three Leeming squadrons with the modified jets so as to alleviate any maintenance problems. Cruising at high level over the North Sea and closing on a VC10K1 tanker during a break in a CAP sortie, ZE966 exhibits the fin-length radar absorbent material (RAM) applied during the upgrade – this particular modification is the easiest way to differentiate a Stage One airframe from a baseline jet. This aircraft was one of the first modified F.3s delivered to Leuchars, joining No 43 Sqn as GF in early 1990. As such, it was transferred to Leeming in August of that year to receive further Gulf upgrades prior to being despatched to Dhahran as DZ. However, its place was taken by ZE200, formerly of No 229 OCU, and ZE966 stayed in North Yorkshire – the new DZ was retained at Leeming as a 'spare' in any case. As can be clearly seen in this shot, ZE966 eventually became DZ with No XI Sqn on a permanent basis after the Gulf War

Above In April 1992 No XI Sqn headed east to the sunny skies of Akrotiri for our annual Armaments Practice Camp (APC). Having completed yet another successful sortie on the towed banner, Flt Lt 'Mork' Graham formates with me as we cross the rugged Cypriot coastline. In this clean configuration, with the wings swept forward at 25°, the F.3's performance at as low a level as possible is very impressive, the aircraft quite comfortably sustaining a high G turn against something like a Hawk – a combination of engine reheat and activation of the Manoeuvre Device System (MDS), which deploys combat slats and flaps, makes the F.3 a serious proposition in a turning fight down low. Infact, the aircraft's edge of the envelope manoeuvrability is only limited by the built-in Spin Prevention and Incidence Limiting System (SPILS), which stops the angle of attack (AoA) building up to a point whereby the F.3 departs from controlled flight. Indeed, SPILS has worked so well that I've never heard of an F.3 pilot who has departed through over-stressing or pulling on too much AoA during ACM – this compares markedly with the Lightning and Phantom FGR.2, both of which would often depart during rigorous combat manoeuvring

Right This unusual photograph was taken from the top of a Hardened Aircraft Shelter (HAS) at Andøya air base in northern Norway during September 1992 whilst No XI Sqn participated in Tactical Fighter Meet 92. The F.3 was departing on a joint CAP sortie with Royal Norwegian Air Force (RNAF) F-16s from Skvadron (Skv) 338, who had also forward deployed to Andøya from their base at Ørland. We were providing 'Red Air' in the meet against raids of RNAF, RAF and *Marineflieger* strike aircraft who were flying up the coast from Bodø, 200 miles to the south of us. Our job was to protect Andøya, using our BVR capability to tackle the front formations of any big attacking packages, whilst Skv 338 would utilise the manoeuvrability of their F-16s in a back-stop role, hitting any jets that managed to get through.

From this angle the wing box and swept back flying surfaces, which have been moved through to 67° to allow the aircraft to fit in the HAS, are very prominent. As mentioned earlier, the pilot soon learns to live without the automatic sweep facility. For example, you quickly realise that the aircraft loses speed and rapidly builds up AoA if you go into a tight turn with the wings swept. Therefore, having attempted this manoeuvre a few times you soon remember to check your speed as you hit the turn, and if you are within the correct limit you can just push the sweep handle fully forward. There is a clutch on the handle itself which you depress to slam the wings forward – it then takes about 11 seconds for them to travel from the 67° to 25° position. The aerodynamic limits for the wings are generous, the F.3 being able to motor along at 450 kts with the surfaces swept fully forward and at over 800 kts in the 67° position. Rarely do you chase anybody at speeds in excess of 480 kts, so the extended wing area allows you to take advantage of the front slats and rear manoeuvre flaps through the MDS if you get into a turning fight

Above Andøya is surrounded by large rocky outcrops which serve to hide the austere forward operating base very effectively. Operating over unfamiliar territory which is quite rugged in its topography requires a variety of different skills not usually used when back at Leeming. For example, you have to be careful not to race head long down a fjord at a great rate of knots, only to find yourself face-to-face with a sold wall of rock at the end. More time spent studying the flight maps prior to launch is essential as much of our day-to-day flying at Leeming is done over water, and there aren't too many 6000-ft high islands in the middle of the North Sea! Many of the fjords are also criss-crossed by high tension wires, which further add to the risk of low-level flying at high speed. You have to be aware of your height in relation to the topography so that you can be confident when it comes to manoeuvring in combat – the minimum pull through height for a loop is a particularly important figure to bury in the back of the brain for future reference.

We acquitted ourselves well in Norway as none of our

opponents had a BVR capability; a BVR fighter pitted against a non-BVR fighter (an AIM-9L-equipped F-16 for example) proved to be a very real threat to the attacking 'mud movers'. Although the F-16 is *the* fighter when it comes to ACM, I'd feel much happier going into combat strapped into an F.3 which boasts the ability to down a Fighting Falcon with a 'Fox One' at a distance of 20 miles. The exercise in Andøya was handled as if we were deploying for war, with eight jets being sent so as to allow six to be constantly available for CAP duties and two on routine servicing.

Between eight and ten crews accompanied the jets, allowing for some flexibility on the operations front. Only operationally-rated pilots and navigators can be sent on a Tactical Fighter Meet, so this narrows the choice of crews down somewhat prior to leaving Leeming. During the two weeks leading up to our departure, the crews chosen for the det were put through a rigorous phase of fighter affiliation against types we could expect to encounter during the exercise

Above I joined No 23 Sqn from the OCU in November 1988, and at that time the squadron was still receiving its jets directly from Warton, having only been established on the first of the month at Leeming. This photograph of ZE833 was taken two months later as Flt Lt Ian McDonald Webb and I were performing an ACM sortie against a brace of Hawk T.1As temporarily seconded to the unit as target aircraft, pending the arrival of more F.3s. These types of flights helped me work up the ladder from 'limited combat ready' to 'fully combat ready' during the course of 1989. After about 50 hours flying time with a frontline unit you are ordained to have reached the latter level of proficiency, although it takes a good 250 to 300 hours on-type in the logbook to feel at one with your aeroplane. Sadly, as part of the 1993 UK Defence White Paper No 23 Sqn was axed, with its final disbandment taking place in March 1994. The F.3 fleet will be limited to 100 aircraft from now on, with the surviving six squadrons operating 13 instead of 15 jets each. ZE833 was the first Tornado F.3 lost by the RAF, the aircraft crashing into the North Sea on 21 July 1989 – its pilot, Flt Lt Steve 'Alf' Moir (a former No 5 Sqn Lightning mate), was killed in the accident

Above Having six months experience under my belt with the 'Red Eagles' of No 23 Sqn, I was one of a handful of crews posted across the base to the newly arrived No 25(F) Sqn in July 1989 – this move gave the new squadron a cadre of pilots and navigators already familiar with both the F.3, and Leeming's HAS procedures, around which to build a fully operational outfit. Prior to it receiving F.3s, the squadron had operated Bloodhound Mk 2 surface-to-air missiles for the past 27 years, its last manned fighter type being the Javelin FAW.9, which it had retired at Leuchars on 30 November 1962!

By the time I reached my fourth frontline squadron in 11 years of service, my reputation as a photographer had preceded me, and I was 'employed' by the unit to shoot a variety of shots in 1990 for No 25(F) Sqn's 75th anniversary. Then the following year Archie Neill and Jim Brown were awarded the title of Tornado F.3 display crew for the 1991 airshow season and I photographed their specially marked jet for the publicity hand-out that accompanied their nationwide performances. This full

afterburner shot was taken during pre-season work-ups on one of the specially generated photo shoots. The Tornado F.3 in full 'burner' is a little slower on initial acceleration than either the Phantom FGR.2 or the Lightning F.6, but it will keep on going all the way up to and past 800 kts. Obviously, as jets get older they tend to get slower as bits are stuck on them and the engines wear out, and by the time I flew the Lightning F.6 its straight line speed was restricted to 625 kts, which was quite a sensible limit in view of the fact that most of the jets were slightly bent! You had to have a firm grip on the rudder, and move the control column to all four corners of the cockpit, just to keep the jet pointing straight and level at the top end of the speed scale at low altitude!

Above right During my time as an air defence pilot, I have been fortunate enough to experience the total revolution in capability that has taken place over the past ten years in terms of the RAF's effectiveness in performing this vital task. Its ability to police the

UK Air Defence Region was greatly improved throughout the late 1980s as the last Lightning F.6s and Phantom FGR.2s were replaced by Tornado F.3s. The final piece in the puzzle was not put in place until early 1991, however, when No 8 Sqn retired its last Shackleton AEW.2s, and received brand new E-3D Sentry Airborne Warning and Control System (AWACS) aircraft in their place. The biggest improvements that I initially experienced with the new AWACS was its ability to track targets over land, a task that was impossible with either the Lightning or the Shackleton. The Sentry is also capable of passing on information concerning other groups of targets some distance away from your immediate threat. The old Shackleton was limited by its radar to covering one target at a time, normally over the sea.

The E-3D's endurance is also impressive, the jet being able to stay on station for as long as the galley meals hold out! Many of the new AWACS crews are ex-fast jet navigators, and with no disrespect to the Shackleton controllers, they know exactly the sort of information you require. With three radios on which to

communicate, you only need to receive key words from the AWACS, rather than a trio of voices giving you information you don't require. The E-3Ds also carry fighter controllers amongst their crew of 17. These improvements combine to give you a clear picture of what it is you are up against.

The subject of this shot was involved in a tragic accident barely weeks after we had formated with it following a routine CAP sortie over the North Sea. WR965 was participating in a maritime exercise involving F.3s from Nos 25(F) and 5 Sqns, amongst others, in the Benbecula area to the west of mainland Scotland on 30 April 1990. In between periods on station, the crew had planned to carry out continuation training, which included a visual approach to Benbecula airfield. As the aircraft closed on the small RAF station, the weather began to deteriorate so the pilot radioed Benbecula Air Traffic Control and told them that he was aborting his approach. Soon after, the Shackleton flew into a cloud-shrouded 823 ft hill on the Isle of Harris, killing its ten-man crew instantly

Above and right A sight now consigned to history – an armed QRA Tornado F.3 from No 25(F) Sqn monitors a former Soviet Tupolev Tu-142 *Bear-F* 'Mod 3' ASW patrol aircraft as it cruises over the North Sea at high altitude. This was my second intercept of an 'enemy' aircraft in two days (my only previous *Bear* experience up to that point had occured 12 months earlier), and it came most unexpectedly during a quiet spell in Russian traffic in mid June 1991. The sortie was quite unusual because Leeming scrambled both QRA aircraft, the second jet following the first after the initial contact had been made. This was due primarily to the fact that the Tu-142 stayed in our patrol zone for a long period of time before being passed over to the Iceland F-15s of the 57th FIS.

When on QRA, the crews are constantly updated on any threats that could enter our area of responsibility. These high flying patrol aircraft are usually picked up by the Norwegian Air Force's F-16s as soon as they leave Russian airspace, and word of an interception is quickly passed onto us. This normally gives us time to don our survival suits and plan the up-coming launch. However, on occasion the first thing you know about the mission taking place is when the hooter sounds and you're running for your jet. Both QRA F.3s are started up inside the HAS just in case one goes U/S, and whichever crew is ready first is despatched and vectored onto the target. At the same time that this is taking place the alert tanker at Brize Norton will also be scrambled and the various GCI stations in the area informed of the mission. The F.3 is the final link in a very big and effective chain that keeps the UKADR clear of threats at all times

Above As the primary task of a QRA crew in peace-time is to identify and shadow the threat, the climb to height is usually performed at a speed of around 400 kts. In theory, the F.3 could reach the *Bear*'s typical cruising altitude of 35,000 ft in under two minutes from 'wheels in the well', but this would leave the crew embarassingly short of endurance once alongside the aircraft. This is particularly true when you take into account that the unidentified contact must be intercepted on the edge of the UKADR, and escorted around its expansive periphery. This mission saw me airborne for four-and-a-half hours, whilst the sortie two days previously occupied four hours of daylight shadowing and three hours on the radar at night. Two days after this sortie we flew another two-hour QRA scramble.

The ex-Soviet Naval Aviation (AV-MF) and Air Force Long-Range (V-VS) Tu-95s and -142s make for huge radar targets, their multi-blade contra-rotating props illuminating the aircraft from many miles away. Once up alongside a *Bear*, the distinctive whine of its four Kuznetsov NK-12 turboprop engines can be clearly heard through the canopy. Turning with a *Bear* can also provide you with the odd memorable moment as the aircraft's

huge wing span (167 ft) allows it to manoeuvre with ease at these rarified heights. In a fully armed and tanked up wide span (45 ft wings spread) F.3 you have to make judicious use of the afterburners to stay in position. Their fighter-type speeds of just under 500 kts also take some getting used to. Despite all the 'scary stories' of the early days when *Bear* crews supposedly shone torches at the pilots of intercepting jets during night missions, or tried to stall turn aircraft into the sea, the only things I ever saw waved at me from an AV-MF Tu-142 were the odd sandwich or two, and occasionally a Zenit camera! This aircraft was one of a pair of *Bear-F*s intercepted on 19 June 1991, the second Tupolev keeping a separation distance of three to four miles. Their ability to turn and change course headings as a pair was most impressive, and we tracked them for over an hour. This intercept was one of the last performed by Leeming's QRA flight. Some years later I was fortunate enough to meet a Russian Bear pilot at an International Air Tattoo, and we spoke of our past encounters. Whilst recounting his experiences he opened his case and pulled out two black and white photographs; one featured a No 111 Sqn Phantom FG.1 and the

other a NoXI Sqn Lightning F.6. Both were of mediocre quality, and I wondered whether this was due to the *Bear's* engine vibration, or because the intercepting pilots were too close to the Tupolev for him to focus on them!

Defending the UKADR is the culmination of many years hard training by an interceptor crew, and to be actually vectored onto a *Bear* is often down to luck. I've known guys who have flown for 20 years and never seen a thing, whilst others who've been on the squadron for a couple of months have pulled their first QRA slot and been scrambled within half an hour onto two *Bears*! Qualification for QRA is one of the first tasks tackled by a new crew on the squadron, as the actual flying is not as taxing as an air combat sortie. Tests for night and day visual identification, and a thorough understanding of the rules and regulations pertaining to interceptions of foreign aircraft, must be completed prior to a QRA rating being issued and the crew pulling its first alert

Above When arriving over the airfield once again after a successful sortie the first thing you must do is make sure that you have joined the runway in use. Circuit height limitations also vary, as does the direction you break into the pattern. The safety of all live weapons prior to returning to terra firma is also a crucial check that needs to be correctly performed. From an airmanship stand point, you must make sure that you know in which direction the wind is blowing, as a tail wind can drastically affect your braking distance, and the time to find that out is not when you're rolling down the runway still doing 150 kts! The 'break' is based on a one- or two-second separation, which is briefed prior to launching. It can be a level break from 800 ft, as photographed here, or a break that sees you climb up to 1250 ft to give the formation elements more separation.

This rapid procession of overhead arrivals and landings stems back to the Vietnam conflict when large numbers of jets needed to land as quickly as possible following long combat sorties. In the Tornado you enter the overhead at 450 kts, pitch into the break and from there it's about 30 seconds until you are down to 150 kts, with gear and flap extended, lined up for landing

Above and left Artistic use of the low winter sun has highlighted both the shape of the F.3 and the dramatic cloud formations often encountered at this time of year. Interceptor crews usually perform 20 per cent of their annual flying at night, and although dedicated night sorties are flown, some day missions during the winter months can see an aircraft launched in daylight and recover at 5.30 pm, having spent the last hour or so in the dark. During the summer, when it stays light well into the evening, crews often only fly the minimum numbers of hours to retain a currency. After 11 pm straight in approaches only are flown at Leeming, and crews are advised to make minimum use of thrust reversers, thus helping the station keep on side with local residents.

I'm not overly keen on night flying as it tends to be very boring. Granted, it's excellent for improving your radar skills, but you never see other aircraft and you tend to spend much of the time head-down in the cockpit. Night tanking is something else, however, particularly when other jets are on the hose, or already holding in the pattern. Set approach procedures then come into play, and you try to acquire a visual ident on the other aircraft in the area. However, it tends to be particularly dark out over the North Sea in winter! ECM missions are often performed at night, and intercepts on blacked out targets are flown as the pinnacle of a night work-up phase for a crew prior to them being deemed fit to perform QRA duties. You have to close on radar to within 300 ft of the contact, whilst making sure that either the navigator or the pilot is constantly head-down monitoring the scope. You then try and acquire the aircraft visually – sometimes you can use moonlight to your advantage, or perhaps you may be equipped with Night Vision Goggles. Occasionally some nights are so dark out over the North Sea – no moon or stars – that all you can do is hold position at 200 yards behind the target and shadow it

Above Neatly lined up alongside the refuelling pipes at Decimomannu in Sardinia in June 1990, six No 25(F) Sqn F.3s are replenished at the end of a hectic day's ACM flying against Bitburg F-15Cs. Squadrons visit the Air Combat Manoeuvring Instrumentation (ACMI) range at Deci once every two to three years and it is considered to be one of the highlights of a frontline tour. Seven aircraft, eight aircrews and 90 technicians are usually despatched for a solid fortnight of top quality ACM work against both fellow F.3s and dissimilar types from Germany, Italy, the USA and the RAF

Right Further east, but still in the Med, this unusual photograph was taken in July 1989 on a baking flightline at Akrotiri during No 23 Sqn's first Armament Practice Camp (APC) with the F.3.

The makeshift canopy covering is actually a parachute, which has been draped over the open cockpit to reduce the heat build-up. The summer was so hot that year that the canopy frames were actually distorting and refusing to lock and seal properly prior to take-off. The sturdy 'ironmongery' of the extended airbrakes shows up extremely well from this angle. These devices are never used on the F.3, a pilot who flies a well executed approach and recovery to land being able to rely purely on the thrust reversers and wheel brakes. In contrast to the Tornado, the Lightning was always landed with the airbrakes deployed, thus allowing the pilot to make an approach with a higher RPM setting. This in turn meant that the thrust available was significantly increased, making it easier for the pilot to overshoot should the need arise

Left The hot weather factor in Cyprus does take some getting used to, and in the worst months between May and August, squadrons on APC have to restrict the number of sorties being flown. The Americans have much stricter rules about hot weather flying primarily because of their more frequent exposure to the dangers of it. At places like Luke or Nellis, only one sortie per day is flown per pilot when the temperature goes above 90°C. Furthermore, if the jet goes U/S on the ground after the crew have strapped in their mission is scrubbed because of their exposure to the high ramp-level heat. Luckily, the F.3's built-in air conditioning (AC) system is well up to the job of keeping you cool on the ground, so once the aircraft is powered up I tend to shut the canopy at the earliest possible moment and let the AC do the work.

The pre-flight ritual is a two-man affair on the F.3, the navigator performing a number of priming duties like firing up the APU, checking out the front cockpit engine igniters and generally arranging the switchology in preparation for the pilot's arrival. I will be signing for the jet whilst this is taking place, checking the airframe Form 700, or log book, for outstanding defects. Having signed for the £20 million fighter, my next task is to perform an airframe walkaround, checking for dents and cracks that the groundcrew may not have picked up, oil or fuel leaks beneath the fuselage or evidence of a birdstrike from the previous flight. The radome attachment points are carefully examined; the tyres checked for excessive wear and cuts; the engine intakes looked at in search of the forgotten spanner or bolt; the wingtip navigation light bulbs flashed up to ensure serviceability; any external ordnance checked for cracked guidance fins; each missiles' coolant supply properly replenished; the flaps examined for dents and oil leaks; the brake pipes visually checked within the wheel wells; and the fire extinguishers looked at to ensure that they haven't been fired off. The jetpipes are also checked for stray bits of metal, which, if present, might indicate a blade failure. The last thing the crewman does before finally strapping in is to ensure that all the ejection seat pins are stowed in the right place

In this close-up shot, No 25(F) Sqn navigator Flt Lt Chris Payling primes his radar whilst his pilot is helped with his straps up front. The high-resolution, multi-function, TV 'tabs', and their associated control keypads, are bolted into the rear cockpit directly in front of the navigator, thus allowing him to readily keep a track of all the necessary data that is inputed into the jet's computer prior to launch

Above The WKA Mauser 27 mm cannon gets a thorough working out on the banner whilst on an APC, the tell-tale cordite smudges around the weapon's breech being a sure sign of sorties flown against No 100 Sqn's Hawk T.1 target towing aircraft. Combined with a rigorous flying programme that sees the same F.3 performing up to four missions a day – and associated thrust-reverser landings – the usually pristine Tornado soon ends up looking like this. These scruffy F.3s were photogrpahed on the ramp at the end of No 25(F) Sqn's four-week long APC in November 1991, the jets having had their external tanks refitted for the flight back to Leeming. We were still waiting for airways clearance to return to the UK at this point so some pilots left it until the very last moment to strap in, trying to catch the last rays of sunshine prior to returning to the drab autumn weather in England.

A total of ten jets are usually despatched on an APC by the squadron in three waves from Leeming, a single airframe in deep maintenance usually being left back at base. We often route through Sigonella, in Italy, on our way down, and as soon as we

arrive at Akrotiri the tanks are taken off and stored for the duration of our stay. The first couple of days are spent shooting video-film on set attack patterns against the Hawk. Then, once the weapons instructors are happy that you're safe, you are cleared to fly about ten air-to-air live gunnery missions. This culminates in an operational shoot where you meet the Hawk head-on. At the merge he either breaks left or right through 540°, and by fair means or foul you have to get onto the banner and shoot off your 100 rounds. Unlike the Lightning, where two jets took it in turns to work the banner in a figure of eight pattern, only one F.3 fires at the target at a time, thus reducing the possibility of a collison. The jet's radar-ranging gunsight helps even mediocre marksmen achieve better scores than the best sharp-shooters from the F.6 days! Half-hour sorties on the banner are the norm, and all gunnery requirements for a unit for 12 months are performed whilst on an APC – virtually no gunnery work on F.3s is undertaken in the UK because of the unpredictable weather. Good visibility and a distinct horizon are the pre-requisites for a successful air-to-air gunnery sortie

Above Arguably the most colourful F.3 scheme to take to the skies was that worn by No 229 OCU's 1990 display jet. Photographed over Northumberland soon after ZE907 had first taken to the skies in its distinctive colours, the aircraft performed on the airshow circuit until August when it was sent back to Leeming for upgrading to Stage One specs. Stripped of its stripes, and boasting various new modifications, the F.3 flew with the *Desert Eagles* from Dhahran throughout the conflict. On this particular sortie, flown in April 1990, we had been acting as a target for the OCU crew to hone their long-range intercept skills against. Frontline units rarely fly mixed sorties with the OCU, the Coningsby-based squadron conducting all of its Tornado F.3 conversion training strictly in-house.

The only contact an operational outfit will have with the OCU is when standardisation instructors (QWIs and QFIs) observe the squadron's mission readiness and general airmanship during their annual inspection. All pilots and navigators fly at least one normal sortie with them, during which time they will throw in an emergency or two to test out your ability to cope with the unexpected. Depending on your experience you may receive a thorough workout if you're a new guy, but then again they may reserve this for an 'old hand'. An oral exam on the aircraft's systems follows after landing, this test usually containing at least one really obscure question pertaining to the F.3, or its systems, to test your depth of knowledge about the aircraft. Operational procedures which may have changed over the past 12 months are also examined thoroughly, thus ensuring that you are up to speed with all aspects of the jet, and its frontline application

The Gulf

Left The Gulf War episode came as unexpectedly to RAF Leeming's Tornado community as it did to the rest of the world, the initial F.3 force on the ground at Dhahran being made up of a dozen aircraft from Nos 5 and 29 Sqns who were in the process of changing over during an APC at Akrotiri at the time. They arrived on 11 August 1990, and from that point on the clock was ticking back in North Yorkshire to ready 18 aircraft to 'Stage One' specs to replace the 'baseline' jets of No 5 (Composite) Sqn. Recently delivered F.3s that had barely had time for squadron markings to be applied to them flew in from Leuchars and Warton. Crews chosen from all three Leeming-based squadrons had a fortnight in which to prepare for the deployment, and come to grips with their dramatically upgraded F.3s. This task was made all the more difficult by the fact that only a handful of modified jets were initially available.

Some of the changes, like the adoption of the AA-standard Foxhunter AI.24 radar which incorporated better visual target-acquisition modes and target lock capabilities, increased cooling for its various 'black boxes' and uprated ECM memory, had been built into the jets at Warton. Further mods added by BAe included the installation of an F/A-18-type HOTAS (Hands On Throttle and Stick), improvements to the Marconi Hermes RHWR (Radar Homing and Warning Receiver) and the ability to boost the engines' power by five per cent through the use of a switch mounted in the cockpit near the throttle which overrode the RB.199 Mk 104s' top-temperature controller.

The addition of Tracor AN/ALE-40(V) flare dispensers on the rear of the jet, and radar absorbent materal (RAM) on the leading edges of the fin, wing and weapons pylons was performed at both Leeming and St Athan. Furthermore, crews had to become familiar with Raytheon-built AIM-9M Sidewinders bought specially for the Gulf to replace Bodenseewerk AIM-9Ls. Phantom FGR.2s and F-4Js from Nos 56 and 74 Sqns were temporarily based at Leeming throughout this period to act as low-level targets for us. We also had lengthy briefings about the capability of the Iraqi Air Force, both in terms of its aircraft and its ground-based missile threat.

By the time I took this photograph on 17 January 1991 my tour of duty in Saudi Arabia had ended, and I was performing readiness sorties in case we were needed as replacement aircraft/crews once the shooting war began in earnest. We trained with the aircraft stored up in a similar configuration to those out at Dhahran, although the live missiles were usually left behind – of course the ambient air temperature of Saudi Arabia was also a little difficult to simulate in mid-January at Leeming!

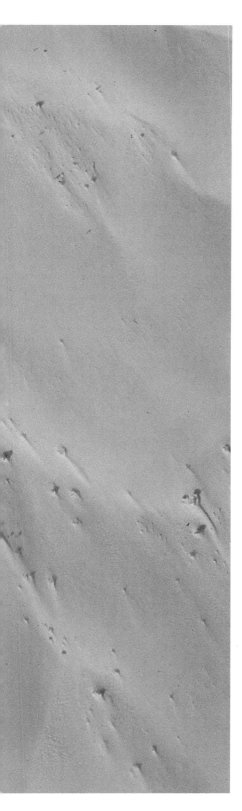

Above A typically sunny day on the No XI Sqn ramp in August 1990 as the 'big push' continues in earnest. We had to fly in all weather due to the limited time available for the work-up, so the groundcrew were subjected to some very harsh weather conditions on the line. Of the 26 aircraft pooled for the *Desert Eagle* detachment, no less than ten of them hailed from newly-activated No 43 Sqn at Leuchars, the unit having only been declared fully operational on 1 July 1990 – the 'Fighting Cocks' flew their Scottish coop and headed south less than six weeks later! ZE161 GI was re-coded DN within No XI (Composite) Sqn and retained, along with another five modified F.3s, in ready reserve at Leeming. I flew 15 hours on pre-deployment work-ups (usually one sortie per day) as one of four crews selected from No 25(F) Sqn for the det – a similar number were assigned from Nos XI and 23 Sqns as part of the new composite unit to replace No 5 (Composite) Sqn

Left Sqn Ldr Ian Howe practices at being a Tornado GR.1 over the vast sea of shifting sand that makes up much of Saudi Arabia, the aircraft cruising along at 500 kts barely 250 ft above the desert. His jet is fully armed up with a quartet of AIM-9Ms and SkyFlash, and the two huge 2250 l external tanks have restricted the wing sweep to 63° rather than 67° – the big tanks also kept the available g-pull down to 2.75 when full, and the distance required to turn a fully fuelled F.3 in this configuration covered a very large patch of desert. I flew a jet into Dhahran from Akrotiri on 29 August 1990, and my first real experience of the size of this undertaking was seeing a 'Berlin Airlift' style corridor of Starlifters, Hercules and Galaxies flying into and out of Dhahran. We actually began overtaking a seemingly endless stream of transports half an hour before we landed in Saudi Arabia

Below Our two weeks of solid training back in the UK was immediately put to the test as soon as we flew in to Dhahran, crews undertaking four-and-a-half hour CAP sorties usually the day after their arrival. This was primarily due to the high threat level that still existed at the time. However, by the end of September when it became obvious that the Iraqis weren't going to push on into Saudi Arabia, we began to undertake training missions as well as our daily CAPs. This was primarily because continual patrol work tended to blunt other aspects of your combat readiness – on CAP all you would do was cruise around at medium altitude in a 'racetrack' pattern listening to AWACS fighter controllers. The only relief from this extremely tedious routine was when you rendezvoused with a VC10 tanker at the mid point in your sortie.

Joining me on this patrol was the No 23 Sqn pairing of Flt Lts Mike Heaton (navigator) and Ian Macdonald-Webb, and the photograph was taken as we joined up for our return to Dhahran after completing another flight over north-central Saudi Arabia.

It was whilst flying around on finals a few weeks into our deployment that I realised I had my throttles near to full power just to turn into the landing pattern! This was due primarily to the weight factor involved with carrying eight live missiles. In a shooting war the first thing you would do is blow the big tanks off, thus returning the F.3 to the world of 7g manoeuvring. Crews talked about lightening the missile load, but in reality you wouldn't have time to ditch ordnance – I for one certainly wouldn't want to throw away a serviceable missile ten miles from the merge in any case!

A SkyFlash weighs in at 425 lbs per round and an AIM-9M at 190, so the combined weight of all this ordnance was no less than 2460 lbs. This figure contrasts markedly with that usually experienced during routine flying at Leeming, where most flights are undertaken with the jets boasting little more than a Sidewinder acquisition round under the wing – we are, however, exposed to something near to the Dhahran fit when on QRA alert back in the UK

Above Of the many photographs I took during my time in the Gulf the sequence featuring the flare deployment are probably the most famous – I won the RAF's 1991 air-to-air photography prize with this shot! The jet with the large tanks was flown on this occasion by Sqn Ldr Ian Howe, and credit for positioning the aircraft in just the right spot goes almost entirely to him. I had an 18 mm Nikon lens fitted to my camera specially for this sortie, and we talked through the varous formating cues prior to launching. We were travelling at 450 kts in close formation and that essentially meant that the flare was being propelled out of the dispenser at that velocity. This gave me only a millisecond in which to capture its spectacular launch on film, and we decided that our best chance of achieving this would be if he broke away from me very slowly, whilst simultaneously moving forward and holding the bank

Right The scabbed on Tracor AN/ALE-40(V) dispensers are clearly visible in this underbelly shot, the 15-round containers being mounted to the rear fuselage engine access doors in a similar fit to the Saudi F.3s, which boasted flares from delivery. The RAF originally specified a flare dispenser fit from new with the ADV variant of the Tornado, but a shrinking budget placed the bolt-on extra firmly on the 'wish list' for the first few years of the F.3's in-service career. However, the possibility of a shooting war developing in the Gulf saw the devices rapidly purchased and bolted onto the *Desert Eagle* Stage One aircraft.

This equipment was new to all the F.3 crews sent to the Gulf, and to check the operability of the system on the way out to CAP, the pilot would usually fire off a couple of flares to ensure that the kit was working as advertised. One of the main differences between operations in the Gulf as opposed to peace-time flying was that an aircraft had to be 100 per cent serviceable for it to be cleared for a CAP mission, whereas at Leeming, sorties would still be undertaken with a minor write-up or two on the Form 700. This particular aircraft is carrying a pair of smaller 1500 l external tanks as borrowed by No XI (Composite) Sqn from the Muharraq- and Tabuk-based Tornado GR.1 communities, hence their unusual colour. Restricted to subsonic speed due to their composite construction, these tanks did allow the pilot to pull up to 5g whilst fitted and still containing fuel, however. An aircraft with 2250 l tanks could only achieve a similar figure when they were empty. The smaller store was used exclusively during training missions, which were usually flown 200 miles south of Dhahran over the 'GAFA' – 'Great Arabian . . . . not a lot (!) Desert'

Right Once No XI (Composite) Sqn had set itself up in Dhahran and established a regular routine of operating procedures, we began flying training missions with the Tornado GR.1 squadrons based a few miles away from us at Muharraq, Bahrain International Airport. They were rehearsing low-level strike missions over the vast wastelands of southern Saudi Arabia, and we would act as attacking fighters, hitting them at any time as they ran in to or away from their objective. This provided both parties with realistic training in an environment that was geographically similar to that encountered by Tornado crews after 17 January 1991. We would usually reform after the sortie had been completed and return to base in a loose formation at medium level. All our training sorties by day or night involved the Muharraq GR.1 force, these jets hailing from Nos 31 (DL code) and 15 (EG) sqns respectively. In peace-time up to 50 per cent of our sorties see us flying as friend or foe for Tornado GR.1s and Jaguar GR.1As as part of a mutual training effort.

Already beginning to show signs of wear and tear, particularly around the tailplane and panel joints, Tornado GR.1 DL, alias ZD790, enjoyed an action filled war with No 31 Sqn, flying no less than 38 combat missions in the 90-day conflict. Part of Muharraq's 'Snoopy Airways' force, the jet boasted garish nose art of a woman named 'Debbie', plus an impressive sortie tally made up of conventional and laser-guided bomb silhouettes

Above Photographed a few months after the end of the Gulf War during a specially arranged photo-shoot out over the North Sea, ZD714 was one of the 84 GR.1/1As that donned 'desert pink' ready for service in the Middle East, although unlike the majority of its Brüggen-based No 14 Sqn contemporaries, it was retained in reserve at RAF Marham. Like the F.3, the GR.1 was retrofitted with updates that had been planned for fitment for several years, budget permitting. Only Germany-based aircraft were chosen due to their engine spec, these GR.1s boasting the higher-rated Mk 103 version of the RB.199 turbofan – the stage 17F single-crystal turbine blades fitted to this version also reduced the chances of the engines overheating due to heat blasted desert dust forming glass deposits that blocked the powerplants' cooling holes. This problem afflicted Saudi Tornado IDSs early on in their service careers.

Surface Wave Absorbant Material and RAM tiles were also added both internally (engine air ducts) and externally (fin, wing and pylon leading-edges). To reduce the chances of patricide an updated Cossor MkXII Mode 4 IFF indentification suite was fitted, allowing greater commonality with American forces in the region. The aircraft's wing-sweep system was also made compatible with the large 2250 l tanks usually only carried by the F.3 force. Nickel-chrome leading-edges were fitted to all Tornado versions as a protective measure against Sidewinder firings, as tests had shown that the original aluminium devices pitted and burnt through after several launches. Finally, and most obvious of all, the jets were resprayed in a highly effective ARTIF (Alkali-Removable Temporary Finish) paint scheme

Above One Tornado that did play its part over Kuwait and Iraq, however, was ZA492 FE, which flew from both Dhahran and Tabuk. Wearing 29 mission symbols and an An-12 *Cub* silhouette beneath its cockpit, this No 16 Sqn jet was heavily involved in anti-airfield sorties with JP233, conventional and laser-guided bombs throughout the conflict. The distinctive sharkmouth became a trademark of the No 16 Sqn-led wing during the deployment, most of the mixed GR.1 fleet at the RSAF base adopting this morale-boosting marking. I was lucky enough to come across this jet during a mid-North Sea refuelling session in early September 1991, having just come off a CAP. By this stage looking extremely well-weathered, but still using 'our' F.3 tanks, ZA492 was photographed only a day or two prior to No 16 Sqn's disbandment which took place that same month. Aside from the large tanks and the mandatory Sky Shadow ECM pod, this jet is carrying a pair of inert 1000-lb bombs. More than 4200 of these weapons (in the live configuration, of course) were dropped by GR.1s during *Desert Storm*

Above This photograph was achieved with great difficulty! I suggested to the powers that be soon after the war ended that it would be an excellent idea to put up a formation that contained a single example of each of the four fast jet types that saw service in the Gulf. My station commander at Leeming, Gp Capt Rick Peacock-Edwards, was keen on the proposal, having himself been deployed to Dhahran literally hours after the conflict started. By April, the availability of jets for the formation was rapidly dwindling as all the 'pink' GR.1s were back in Germany, the Buccaneers were only weeks away from being repainted, a large number of Jaguars were being prepared for deployment to Turkey and most of our F.3s had been resprayed with unit markings.

After many phone calls we finally settled on a time, place and a photoship. My mount for the sortie was a Jaguar T.2 from No 41 Sqn, capably flown by Sqn Ldr Mike Rondot (now retired); the veteran Jaguar GR.1A, with Sqn Ldr Steve Shutt at the controls, came from No 54 Sqn ('White Rose', alias XZ367, flew 40 combat missions); Tornado GR.1 ZD714 flew in specially from No 14 Sqn in Germany, having stayed in reserve during the war, a fate which had also befallen Buccaneer S.2B XV332 from Lossiemouth. No 25(F) Sqn F.3 ZE199 was flown in the slot by Gp Capt Peacock-Edwards, and was chosen because it lacked any unit badge – it too had seen no war service. A close inspection of the tail of this jet does, however, reveal a No 19(F) Sqn zap! The weather for the sortie over Leeming was dreadful that day (16 May 1991) so we had to head out to sea for 50 miles until we found the clear patch of sky the Met office had promised us was there. As a parting shot on this sortie, I owe a great deal of appreciation to all the crews who made the taking of this unique shot possible

Left A No II(AC) Sqn Tornado GR.1A and a No 25(F) Sqn Tornado F.3 kick in the 'burners and break formation for the camera directly in front of my trailing aircraft. The engine thrust levels available in the GR.1 and F.3 vary only slightly to suit their specific mission needs. The Mk 103 is good for about 16,000 lbs in reheat and the Mk 104 16,523 lbs without the extra boost. The F.3 also benefits during peacetime from being much lighter than its bomber counterpart when configured for training sorties

Left After completing the formation shots I photographed the aircraft independently, taking full advantage of the impressive cloudscapes that covered the North Sea that day. I had asked each of the participating units to try and configure their aircraft with representative stores as carried in the Gulf, and of all the jets in the formation, the Buccaneer best reflected its true wartime mission fit – only the starboard inner wing tank, worn in combat to extend the aircraft's already impressive endurance, was missing. The crucial store brought to the Middle East by the 12-strong Buccaneer force sits unobtrusively alongside the AIM-9L – the ageing Westinghouse AN/AVQ-23E Pave Spike pod. This device, originally developed for USAF F-4Ds and Es in the latter stages of the Vietnam War when LGBs were first used, enabled the Tornado force to hit targets like tanks, HASs and bridges with unnerving precision from altitudes in excess of 20,000 ft, but only during the hours of daylight.

A cell of four Tornados would usually be controlled by a pair of Buccaneers, the navigators in the latter jets designating their targets with the pods' laser and guiding the 1000-lb LGBs down an 'imaginery' basket of reflected energy to the impact points. A total of 216 sorties were flown by the dozen Buccaneers in-theatre between 2 and 27 February.

Above On 26 July 1991 I was again fortunate enough to be in the right place at the right time, tagging along with the display pair from No 208 Sqn as they headed back to Lossiemouth from the RAF Brawdy Open Day, held 24 hours before. I too had attended the show, flying in the 'spare' F.3 for Archie Neill, who was performing at the event. Prior to returning east on the Monday morning, I briefed the crews on what I wanted to photograph, and they were more than willing to oblige as they were heading in a north easterly direction in any case.

The grey and green jet had flown the display routine at Brawdy, whilst XV863 (variously known as 'Tannavoulin', 'Debbie' and 'Sea Witch') had stolen the show in the static park. One of the last Buccaneers deployed to Bahrain in February 1991, it flew a handful of missions for the Muharraq and Dhahran Tornado GR.1s. Dedicated designation missions were annotated in black beneath the cockpit, whilst independent bombing sorties, which saw the jet targeting its own LGBs, were marked in red. XV863 is also fitted with a AN/ALQ-101(V)-10 ECM pod on its starboard outer pylon

Above 'Glenmorangie', alias XW530 of No 12 Sqn, diverted into Leeming in December 1991 following an engine surge whilst refuelling from a nearby tanker. The aircraft's suspect Rolls-Royce Spey 101 turbofan was duly replaced with a line unit brought down by a team specially flown in by Hercules from Lossiemouth. This 12-mission veteran was one of the last Buccaneers resprayed in more conventional camouflage, the shockingly stained 'desert pink' sitting comfortably with its battle-hardened reputation as the last 'all-British' jet bomber

Left Just as we helped the Tornado GR.1s in their pre-war work-ups, we also flew a number of affiliation missions with the Muharraq JagDet GR.1As. This pair were photographed at medium level as we cruised back up the coast to Bahrain following a two-hour sortie that consisted in the main of fighter bounces at ultra low-level – we had paused briefly mid way through the mission to rendezvous with a tanker, before commencing hostilities once again. We followed the jets back into Bahrain for a face-to-face debrief and a well earned beer following the end of the training session. One of the Jaguar pilots was a chap by the name of Stu Weatherstone, and I hadn't seen him since he had sold me his car ten years earler at Brüggen – it really is a small world!

The Jaguars were difficult to 'shoot down' over the desert because they flew so low, and acquiring them visually was a nightmare. As an indication of their operational altitude for much of the sortie, I saw flares that were pumped out of the fuselage-mounted AN/ALE-40 pods bouncing onto the desert floor and extinguishing themselves on the sand itself! The Jaguar has always been a favourite jet to 'hassle' with as the aircraft always pitch up on time and on target – rarely do they have to scrub a mission through unserviceability.

The 12-strong JagDet performed wonders in the dedicated Battlefield Air Interdiction (BAI) role assigned to it over Kuwait. No less than 618 sorties were flown during the war against a variety of targets ranging from tanks to naval vessels. These two 'virginous' GR.1s were later christened 'Fat Slags' (XX962) and 'Sadman' (XZ364) respectively, and between them contributed 84 sorties out of the 600+ flown. Both jets are carrying AN/ALQ-101(V)-10 ECM pods

The Falkland Islands

Right Although the Falklands posting is a lonely five-week tour, it does have its positive aspects, not the least of which is operating with old acquaintances from other squadrons within the F.3 community. It also allows you to gauge your own unit's proficiency in relation to other squadrons from say Leuchars or Coningsby. From a photographic standpoint, the No 1435 Flight posting is also a good one to go on as when the weather is fine, the combination of strong sunlight and unspoilt scenery make for some breathtaking backscapes against which to place your subject.

In this shot we are just rounding the southern tip of West Falkland during a routine training sortie at medium altitude, both F.3s being half armed up with four Sidewinder and two SkyFlash missiles apiece. Flying the jets in this configuration is very enjoyable as their rate of turn is quite impressive with the external tanks left off – the cold weather in the South Atlantic also increases the engines' thrust, thus improving its manoeuvrability

Overleaf All sorties are treated as fully operational flights as there are no diversionary fields in the Falklands. Weather reports become crucial down there, because if the weather socks in after you've launched there really is no where else to go! The forecast has to be good for at least two hours before a mission is given the green light. As can be seen in this photograph, the ability to fly at ultra low-level without any restrictions is also highly enjoyable, although one has to keep a wary eye out for the FIGAS (Falkland Island Government Air Service) Islanders, which are painted blood red all over, as they perform their daily taxi service between various settlements. We let them know where we are going to be, and at what time, and they do a similar thing with us, thus avoiding any conflictions.

All of our sorties involve controllers from the three Falkland Islands Air Defence Ground Environment (FIADGE) mountain-top radar sites. The primary location for intercept directing is at Mount Kent, No 303 Surveillance Unit (SU) utilising a Marconi Series 600 (RAF Type 97) radar from their site west of Port Stanley. The posts atop Byron Heights (No 7 SU) and Mount Alice (No 751 SU), both on West Falkland, use the less effective Plessey AR-3D (RAF Type 94) system – a further Type 97 is fitted near Mount Pleasant Airport (MPA). Life on these sites is basic to say the least, and Tornado crews try and boost morale a bit by overflying the controllers at low-level whenever we are in the area. The crew flying at low-level in this shot are Flt Lts Don Morrison (pilot) and Hugh Griffiths (navigator) from No 111 Sqn. We are both at 250 ft heading down 'A-4 Alley' towards San Carlos Water on East Falkland

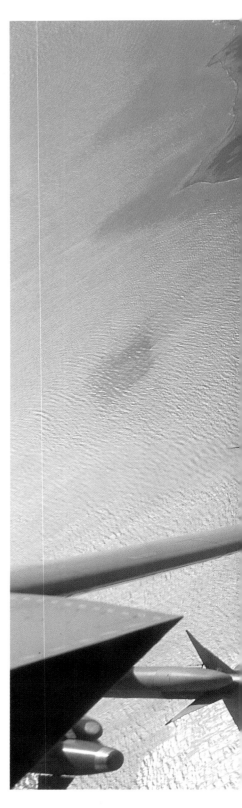

Above One of the best things about the Falklands flying is having your own dedicated Hercules C.1K always on call. The boys from No 1312 Flight organise their sortie around your requirements, so at least one refuelling is undertaken per aircraft on every mission. The Hercules is ideal for the task as it has no real low-level height restrictions. Back in the UK you have to 'tank in the 20s' with the VC10s, which usually means climbing away from your CAP area up to their altitude. In the Falklands, however, it's real 'five star' service, and we usually do a face-to-face brief at MPA prior to launching on the sortie. Most refuelling is done above 1000 ft as the air turbulance below that height tends to whip the drogue around too much. Two C.1Ks are permanently based at MPA, with one aircraft and crew on constant short notice standby in support of the QRA jets. The two Hercules accumulate around 75 hours of flying per month between them in support of the F.3s, a similar figure being achieved by the aircraft during the course of their patrol work over the Falkland Islands Conservation Zone

Right There are a variety of missions that can be flown whilst at MPA, and not all of them see you peforming intercepts or ACM with fellow F.3s. Combat affiliation with the Hercules, or the Sea Kings and Chinooks, for example, is most rewarding, their ability to fly 'low and slow' making for some frantic manoeuvring by a chasing F.3 if a gun or missile kill is to be achieved. A variation on the simple one v one will see an F.3 act as an escort for the Hercules or the helicopters, and the opposing fighters then attempt to repulse the 'invading' force. As can be seen in this chapter, the Flight is yet to mark up two of its F.3s with white tails to distinguish them as the 'bad guys', which they did with their Phantom FGR.2s. This pristine Tornado, which wears the C code on its tail (christened 'Charity' for obvious reasons), was built as one of 46 Batch 6/Block 12 F.3s delivered from October 1987 onwards. It served for almost five years with No 5 Sqn at Coningsby before being selected for service with No 1435 Flight in late 1992

Above Don and Hugh streak over the Limphonia region of East Falkland. Barren and predominantly featureless, this area covers the size of a county and is populated exclusively by walruses. Although many of these beaches look almost Caribbean in appearance, the water temperature seldom gets above 40°F and many of the coves and inlets are still covered in Argentine mines. One of the favourite pastimes of crews whilst flying over East Falkland is the spotting of war wrecks, particularly Skyhawks and Pucaras, which still litter the island. Wearing the famous Maltese Cross and the letter H on its tail, ZE209 is quite an historical aircraft in its own right as it was the first F.3 delivered to No 29 Sqn on 6 February 1987. After a long spell with the Coningsby-based unit, the aircraft moved across the airfield to No 229 OCU in late 1990, from where it was allocated to No 1435 Flight in July 1992

Above Waving the flag for the benefit of the locals, we cruise over Port Stanley itself, with its uninvitingly short runway immediately aft of my wingman. I visited the settlement a couple of times during my stay, and was amazed at how the small 4000 ft-long strip was converted into RAF Port Stanley for the Phantom FGR.2s of No 29 Sqn and the Harrier GR.3s of the No 1453 Flight. Over 6000 ft of AM-2 matting was laid to provide small dispersal sites for the deployed units. An arrestor wire sytem was used by No 29 Sqn throughout their stay on the small strip – this airfield was originally designed around FIGAS's requirements, and they fly the notoriously nimble Islander! To make matters worse for the original interceptor crews, firstly their accommodation was moored alongside that jetty which protrudes into the bay just beneath my wingtip, and secondly, much of the beach area around the airfield was then still heavily mined. In Stanley itself is a superb museum which charts the history of the island, including a large section on the war. Many aircraft parts, including bits from a Pucara and a Skyhawk are on display, and it's well worth a visit if you're in the area!

Above The MPA facility is a vast improvement on 'rugged' Port Stanley, the purpose-built strip first opening for business in May 1985. Each of the four Tornado F.3s has its own hangar built into the undulating terrain which surrounds the base, the shelters being connected to the runway by miles of taxyway. The hills in the distance saw some of the fiercest fighting of the war in early June 1982, the barren scrubland which surrounds MPA offering little protective cover for the advancing British troops

Above Having just completed a routine patrol, ZE812 'Faith' is quickly turned around in readiness for its next flight. The telltale scuffing of the tail denotes that lift-dump landings are the norm at MPA. Aerodynamic braking is also practised regularly so as to ensure that pilots don't rely too much on the buckets. The latter tend to make you very complacent about the aircraft's brakes because they allow you to effectively stop within 2000 ft of touchdown. The buckets and wing lift spoilers will deploy as soon as weight is felt on the undercarriage, the systems being primed by the pilot 'rocking' the throttles outboard just prior to landing – this is what's known in the trade as a PATRL, jargon for a Pre-Armed Thrust Reverse Landing. The buckets are simple and effective, and the only thing you have to keep an eye on is

the engine power setting. If it is too high the buckets will push the aircraft's nose down onto the runway too hard as the F.3 rapidly decelerates.

The jet shakes around a fair bit when the buckets are used, but the nosewheel steering is very effective and it will easily maintain a centre-point. This latter system has high and low gearing settings, so depending on how much you move the rudder pedals, if you are in low gearing the nose will only move a small amount. Conversely, high gearing will allow you to move the wheel a lot, which is ideal for taxying and HAS parking. Therefore, you should always land in low gearing so that any speed shimmy on the wheel won't move the nose gear around too much

Above The groundcrew chock the F.3 whilst the navigator gingerly levers himself out of the back seat. The fuel bowser can just be seen to the left of shot, chugging around to the recently shutdown jet. The live rounds are always left attached to the pylons, thus allowing any serviceable F.3 to be quickly scrambled on a QRA launch. This aircraft, like the other Tornados with No 1435 Flight, lacks the Stage One mods fitted to most of the UK-based F.3s – the leading edges of the wings and tailfin are devoid of RAM, and the Tracor flare boxes are absent from the rear fuselage. ZE812 was allocated to the Flight from No 23 Sqn, where it had previously served for a time as EA. I flew this aircraft on several occasions in January 1989 when it was still new and clean, but by the time we crossed paths once again, four years of frontline flying had left it in less than 'showroom' condition

Left ZE812 is pushed back into its 'hangarette' with the crew still seated in the cockpit. The harsh life that these jets lead in the South Atlantic is shown by the heavy weathering of the wing and taileron leading edges, the paint having been worn down to the primer. Engineers are flown out to the MPA from the UK to perform in-depth maintenance on the Tornados in situ, all but the most comprehensive of overhauls being completed in the Falklands. Any transits to or from the 'mother country' take at least 24 hours to complete, and involve a minimum of two F.3s and a tanker. This greatly reduces the effectiveness of the Flight, so aircraft rotations are kept to a minimum – they only usually occur when a major airframe overhaul is due

Above The small No 1435 Flight crew recreation area has been adorned with a 'stunning' piece of original artwork entitled 'The Goose', in honour of the Upland Goose which inhabits MPA. Each of the caricatures are based on the individual emblems of the eight Phantom FGR.2 units (including the OCU) who contributed crews during the aircraft's decade of service in the South Atlantic. The 'desperate' Phantom FGR.2 is seeing off a snooping Argentine Air Force Boeing 707 with a short burst from its cannon pod. A Tornado mural has also been recently started to highlight the Flight's change of equipment. From a hardware point of view, the crewroom also boasts the front canopy from an Argentine A-4 downed during the war, plus an outer wing panel from one of the recently scrapped FGR.2s. A squadron leader commands the Flight, and only operationally qualified crews are sent down to MPA. Even then, high-time pilots and navigators are normally chosen as minimal supervision is available once in-theatre, and you tend to be your own boss in terms of choosing where and when to fly. The crews only spend four to five weeks at a time in the Falklands primarily because there is no simulator in which to practice other aspects of interceptor flying

Left Despite the thermometer nudging 75°F at times during the summer months, the water temperature remains a constant freezing all year round. Therefore, the crew have to don immersion suits prior to every flight. In this candid photograph, Don Morrison is wearing an internal suit beneath his flying kit and 'speed jeans', whilst Hugh Griffiths is modelling the external type, which covers everything. The distinctive Falkland Islands crest has been hand-painted onto all four No 1435 Flight jets, the overall shape and placement of the unit's markings being virtually identical to those worn on the late-lamented Phantom FGR.2s

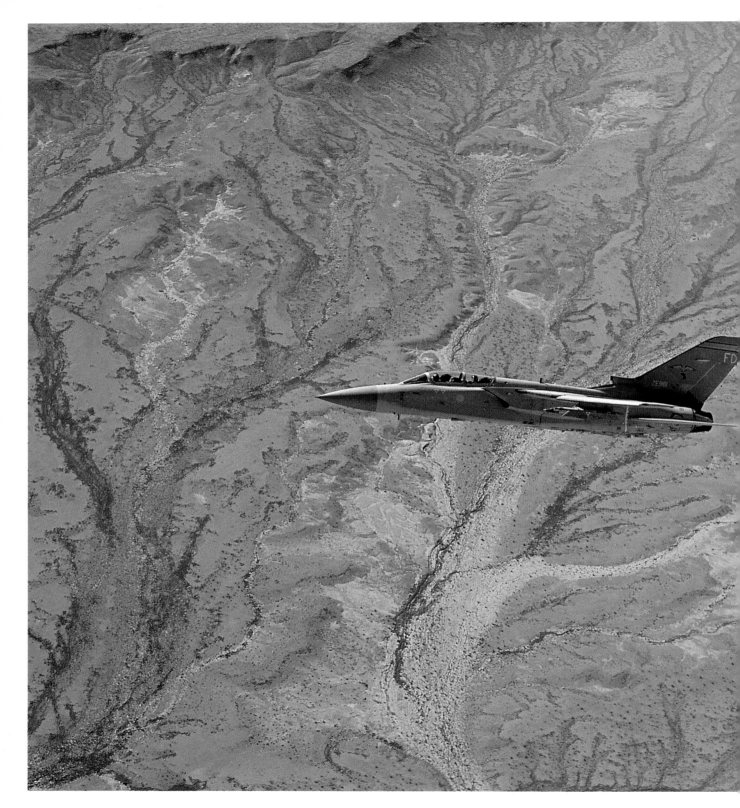

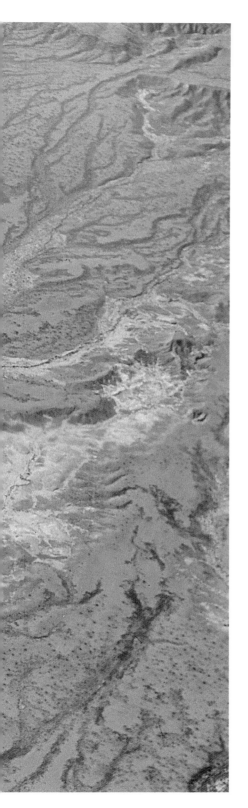

Red Flag 93

Left Few places in the world resemble the lunar landscape of Nevada, and up until October 1992 the graceful lines of a Tornado F.3 had been a rare sight in this 'neck of the woods'. Indeed, *Red Flag 93-1*, which commenced on 13 October 1992 (the US Fiscal year starts on 1 October, hence the confusing exercise title!) marked the F.3's debut at Nellis AFB. Five Stage One-plus jets pooled from each of the squadrons at Leeming, plus a single F.3 from Coningsby-based No 29 Sqn, deployed to Nellis, via Goose Bay, on 5 October, the jets being flown out by No 5 Sqn crews. Aircrew from Nos XI and 29 Sqns also participated in the six-week long exercise, each unit spending a fortnight in Nevada.

The same F.3s stayed in-theatre throughout *Red Flag 93-1*, crews rotating across from the UK as a squadron when their slot arrived. A total of 12 crews were brought over by each unit, this number being the maximum aircrew/aircraft ratio achievable with only six jets deployed. This F.3 was one of a pair 'borrowed' from No 25(F) Sqn, and it was photographed being flown by a No XI Sqn crew at the end of a familiarisation sortie. One Famil Flight was flown by each crew soon after arrival in Nevada, this sortie giving you an idea of the sheer size of the range area that *Red Flag* covered

Overleaf All the external Stage One-plus mods are clearly visible on ZE887 as it cruises over the desert valley area east of Nellis – one slight change is that the Tracor flare pods have been replaced by the less 'draggy' Vinten devices. Delivered from Warton directly to No 43 Sqn in early 1990, this jet was sent to Leeming in August of that year for Gulf modification work. However, the jet was kept back in reserve in North Yorks and it eventually became DJ with No XI Sqn. The F.3 force acquitted itself well in Nevada, the Americans being particularly impressed by the jets' night intercept capabilities with its AA-standard Foxhunter radar. Mission packages launched for the ranges at 1300 and 1800 hours everyday throughout the exercise period, with four Tornado F.3s forming part of the attacking 'Blue Force' which numbered anywhere between 32 to 40 aircraft of mixed types. We were tasked with 'sanitising' the area ahead of our strike package, ensuring that no 'enemy' fighters came anywhere near our bombers. This tasking contrasted markedly with our traditional role of defending the UKADR

Right The actual procedures, or ground rules, involved in a *Red Flag* exercise leave you somewhat overawed to start with, and it's not really until you commence your second week over the ranges that you start to become familiar with how everything runs. As this was the F.3's Nellis debut, all three squadrons involved in the exercise were keen to impress the locals with their prowess in all-weather BVR interceptions. We performed an intensive work-up period prior to the deployment, and a couple of ex-GR.1 navigators on the squadron who had been on *Red Flags* before explained to us how things basically worked over there. Aircrews from Nos 617, II(AC) and 9 Sqns were also involved in *93-1*, flying 'Blue Force' Tornado GR.1s, so they steered us in the right direction as well. The Americans are amongst the best at organising large strike packages, and it was truly amazing to see how much detail our mission planners went into during the sortie briefs. Despite this, the missions flown were relatively uncomplicated and well thought out, virtues which make a *Red Flag* exercise the ultimate training aid.

Preparations for an upcoming flight were commenced the day before the sortie was scheduled to be flown. On mission day, your briefings commenced at 0730 for a 1300 launch, the sortie lasting up to two hours. The rest of the day was devoted purely to debriefing, this task being undertaken by seasoned staff who specialise solely in *Red Flag* exercices. They are all 'old sweats' who have seen every trick in the book tried, and having talked you through your mission, offer you advice at the end of it. What they are looking for is an upward learning curve which charts the lessons you have learnt as the exercise has progressed

Right *Red Flag 93-1* was not all firsts for the RAF, however, as this exercise saw the Victor K.2 complete its final North American deployment. Dedicated purely to the F.3 force, a pair of No 55 Sqn aircraft operated out of Mather AFB, in California, alongside KC-135s who were performing a similar tasking for USAF elements of the exercise. Two air-to-air refuellings were part of each mission (day or night), the F.3s rendezvousing with the Victors before ingressing with the strike package, and then topping up once again on the way back to Nellis. The tankers flew a typical 'racetrack' pattern on the northern edge of the range, but they never actually entered the 'live' area. The No 29 Sqn jet on the starboard hose lacks the RAM covered leading-edge panelling of the other two F.3s, both of which flew with the *Desert Eagles* during the Gulf conflict – it does, however, boast Vinten flare pods beneath the rear fuselage. The 'Plus' part of the 1990 upgrade, which saw the F.3's air conditioning system uprated, canopies modified so as to prevent heat warp and special hot weather tyres fitted to the wheel hubs, came in extremely handy in the dry heat of a Nevada autumn

Above Mission accomplished, my wingman pulls into the break over the green oasis of downtown Nellis, prior to lining up on one of the two live runways which serve the base. Joining the pattern during a *Red Flag* exercise is one of the trickiest things to perform safely whilst on deployment, ATC having strict procedural rules which govern your approaches. No military airfield back in the UK comes close to rivalling Nellis for sheer size, and with hundreds of movements taking place every day, you have to be fairly careful about adhering to arrival times and course directions.

My favourite moment whilst on deployment was 'downing' an aggressor F-16C that was simulating a 'Red Force' Su-27. My navigator and I acquired him visually whilst down on the deck, and pulling the nose up, I took a sneaky 'Fox Two' shot at him before he saw me, thus reaffirming the old adage that 'it's the one you don't see that kills you'. We learnt a huge amount from the pilots at the Adversary Tactics Division, and although they only had eight jets on strength, they gave us real headaches once aloft

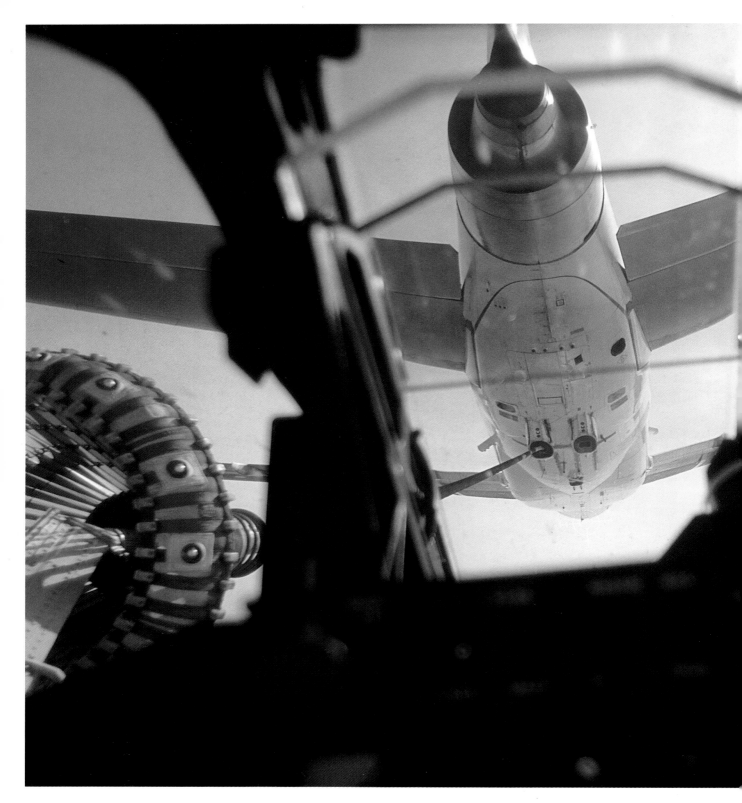

On the tanker

Left The Tornado F.3 is blessed with very 'long legs', particularly if the engines are kept in military power. Even without external tanks fitted, its range on internal fuel only is about 3600 kms, which is considerably greater than any other Western interceptor. Besides its wing and fuselage fuel tanks, the RAF's Tornado force also boasts a fin fuel cell, a unique addition fitted only to the British GR.1 and F.3. However, to prevent the crew having to launch in a jet chocked full of Avtur, the interceptor squadrons rely heavily on the tanker force down at RAF Brize Norton.

Many missions involve at least one air-to-air refuelling bracket, and this segment of the flight is thoroughly briefed prior to the launch. We discuss when we plan to leave the CAP for the tanker, and how many F.3s will refuel at a time – if a four-ship is launching a pair will refuel first whilst the remaining two continue to perform the patrol. The possibility of the tanker being in cloud is also discussed, and the drill for single-point only refuelling talked through. Fuel uploads are also briefed for each aircraft.

Having completed your first spell on CAP, you break away from the patrol line and climb up to the rendezvous point with the tanker, which is usually cruising around in a 'racetrack' pattern at 25,000 ft over the North Sea. Once in visual contact, either a full R/T or silent approach can be made, the fighter positioning itself on the starboard side of the tanker. You are now under his control until the fuel has been passed. In this instance, I am refuelling from a No 216 Sqn Tristar K.2, which boasts a larger drogue basket than the VC10K. Once in position behind the tanker, it's simply a matter of running the probe up a known reference line along the hose until it makes firm contact with the basket.

Firmly plugged in, you fly the F.3 just like you were in close formation, keeping a fix on the 'traffic lights' immediately above the Hose Drum Unit (HDU). The correct overtake speed for positive contact is about five to eight knots – too fast and the probe may buckle and snap, whilst if it's too slow a 'soft contact' will take place, whereby the fuel valve opens but the probe isn't engaged correctly and Avtur flows around the probe and all over the jet instead

Above Prior to the RAF committing itself heavily to operations in the Gulf and over the former Yugoslavia, we used tankers on almost every mission. Now, however, due to the fact that the tanker force is currently smaller than at any time since the early 1960s, we often only see a VC10K during exercises, or when crew proficiency training is required. This isn't too big a problem due to the F.3's range, and you can put bids in to try and secure the support of a tanker if you feel the training benefit derived from its attendance is worthwhile. All new F.3 pilots must complete a 'work-up' phase of day and night air-to-air refuelling, and this always takes priority when its comes to tanker allocation

Left During the large Joint Maritime Co-ordination (JMC) exercise held in February 1992 in the North Atlantic, I was fortunate enough to witness the unusual sight of a tanker refuelling another tanker. The reason behind this was that the VC10K3 had three HDUs from which thirsty F.3s could replenish their tanks, whilst the Tristar K.1 was restricted to the single centre-line unit. Therefore, the No 216 Sqn jet would fly out specially from Brize Norton to refuel the VC10K3, which remained on-station throughout the day, swapping flight crews when required. The Tristar would then return to its Oxfordshire base for more Avtur, remaining on standby until called out once again. Although the Lockheed jet is restricted to a single HDU, it can pass over 136,000 kgs of fuel, as compared to the VC10K3's 80,000 kgs. Due to the invisible 'bow wave' which precedes a large aircraft like a VC10K3, tanker to tanker refuellings are restricted to the centreline Flight Refuelling Mk17B HDU, thus reducing the effects of aerodynamic buffeting

Above Having pulled off CAP during an exercise over the Western Approaches in early 1992, a pair of No XI Sqn F.3s refuel in unison from a No 101 Sqn VC10K2, the jets spending 20 minutes each on the wing-mounted Flight Refuelling Mk32 HDUs. When you arrive on the tanker your jet is usually quite light due to its reduced fuel load, but as the Avtur is rapidly pumped across you can feel the F.3 getting heavier, particularly when you are carrying 2250 l tanks beneath the wings. Therefore, more engine power is required to stay in position, especially when turning at the end of a straight 'racetrack' leg. Once the alloted fuel has been passed, the flow is stopped and the green HDU light changes to flashing amber. This is the signal for the pilot to break contact, so you then reduce engine power by one or two per cent, allowing the F.3 to fall back and the

probe to clear the basket. You can then either pull away and formate on the VC10's port wing, waiting for your wingman to finish receiving his load, or dive back down to patrol height and declare yourself back on CAP.

The aircraft refuelling from the starboard HDU in this shot was in fact the 25th Tornado F.3 delivered to the RAF, making its first flight from Warton on 13 February 1987. Delivered to Coningsby's Aircraft Servicing Flight 11 days later, ZE251 was one of four Block 11 jets that formed the Tornado F.3 Operational Evaluation Unit (OEU) the following April under the command of Wg Cdr Mal Gleave. Due to the OEU's testing brief, its fleet has to consist of the latest delivery spec airframes, so when Block 12 F.3s began leaving Warton in September 1987, ZE251 was transferred back to the OCU. It was from here that No XI Sqn

picked it up during the topsy turvy autumn of 1990, when it seems that most of the frontline F.3 force passed through the squadron's books! This airframe did, however, stay in North Yorks after the war, where it became Delta Echo. In July 1993 ZE251 was transferred to St Athan and placed in long term storage

Above Working with a tanker provides you with an excellent opportunity to photograph other aircraft who may be sharing the refuelling brackets with you. On this mission we were briefed for a half-hour slot in the morning, the VC10K2 then refuelling four Buccaneers S.2Bs from No 208 Sqn, who had been working with us. Once I had topped up my tanks, I pulled back and waited for the strike aircraft to pitch up. With no pressing necessity to get back on CAP, I tagged along for a short while and photographed the mass formation as it turned into sun. The Buccaneer pilots had a reputation of being 'hard chargers' when it came to refuelling, their nose-aligned probe allowing them to hit the basket with unnerving accuracy at an impressive velocity

Above Of all the fast jets in RAF service that are currently capable of tanking, the Jaguar GR.1A is considered to be the most difficult of all to refuel in. This is due primarily to the poor throttle response from its twin Adour Mk 104 turbofan engines, this powerplant delivering its optimum performance at low level. Therefore, to reduce the Jaguar's 'breathlessness', VC10 pilots will often descend to medium altitude (around 10,000 to 15,000 ft), thus shortening the time spent by the strike aircraft climbing to their height. Once plugged in, it's not uncommon to see one of the Jaguar's engines in afterburner, the pilot battling to keep up speed as his internal fuel load increases. We often repeat this performance in the F.3 if the tanker goes into a turn and we are carrying 2250 l tanks plus a full weapons fit, the

engine in 'burner being used as the throttle. Refuelling in afterburner is quite a tricky procedure as it is easy to get your hands out of synchronisation with the constant altering of the throttle controls.

These two Jaguar GR.1As are both carrying empty practice bomb dispensers on the underfuselage stores stations, having dropped their ordnance on Holbeach, in Norfolk, during a low-level strike sortie. Wearing a 'Desert Cats' bonedome, the pilot in XZ111 is from No 6 Sqn, the EL coding denoting this fact despite the jet being otherwise 'markingless', whilst his wingman with the weathered Gulf War tanks is flying a fully marked up No 41 Sqn Jaguar GR.1A. Both aircraft hail from the Jaguar wing at Coltishall in Suffolk

Above Victor XH669 was spared from performing Gulf service with No 55 Sqn in 1990, but it did nevertheless support these No 41 Sqn Jaguars as they deployed to Norway as part of a *Teamwork* exercise earlier that same year. This airframe was infact the oldest surviving Victor B.2R modified into a K.2 – a total of 24 three-point tankers were delivered to the RAF, XH669 being the 18th airframe converted. Throughout its life as a tanker, this aircraft served exclusively with either Nos 55 or 57 Sqns, and due to its rather advanced years in comparison with its ramp mates, the ex-bomber was retired soon after this photograph was taken

Above Now gone, but not forgotten, the Victor K.2s were impressive to work with, their archaic appearance reminding me of the submarine *Nautilus* from the 1960s television series, *Voyage To The Bottom Of The Sea*! Unlike the VC10K crews, who tend to keep the jet in autopilot whilst refuelling, Victor pilots often flew their aircraft manually, which made the job a little more difficult from the receiver's perspective, particularly when you went into the turn. The aircraft possessed the ability to climb with an F.3 in military power, thus revealing its true colours as a converted bomber rather than a former airliner. One of the more challenging things you could do with a Victor didn't involve tanking at all – a procedure called an accompanied let down would see you descending (sometimes in cloud) to land whilst trying to hold formation on the Victor's wing, and at the same

time perform an instrument approach. This routine usually took place during an overseas deployment if you experienced some form of navigational problem in transit. Keeping in the correct position was rather difficult as when he reduced his power by half a percent, you had to lose about 25 per cent of your thrust! Similarly, his airbrakes were almost four times the size of those on the F.3, which of course meant the chances of an overshoot on my part were quite high.

Trailing the hoses from its FR.20B HDUs, this weathered K.2 was retired along with a handful of other survivors when its parent unit, No 55 Sqn, disbanded at Marham on 15 October 1993. A *Desert Storm* veteran, XL164 was christened 'Saucy Sal' and flew 41 missions in support of the Coalition, the tally still being present when this photograph was taken in March 1992

Above The JMC exercise mentioned earlier in this chapter saw No XI Sqn performing its maritime support role in defence of NATO warships, our target intercepts being co-ordinated by shipborne fighter controllers. Our adversaries for much of the exercise were CAF CF-18As from Nos 409 and 439 Sqns, who would fly anti-shipping attacks as well as fighter sweeps in conjunction with other strike assets. On this particular mission, following a torrid four v four session that had seen us repulse the Canadians, we all arrived on the tanker virtually simultaneously. After taking it in turns to replenish our much depleted fuel stocks, I held back with the last of the CF-18As and took the opportunity to capture the moment on film

Strike Command

Left Less than two months away from their deployment to the Gulf, a pair of No 16 Sqn Tornado GR.1s cruise over the far friendlier skies of the Lake District, their crews blissfully unaware of what Saddam had in store for them. This photograph was taken in July 1990 following an affiliation sortie with No 25(F) Sqn Tornado F.3s. Germany-based GR.1s often land away at Leeming whilst flying on low-level sorties in Scotland or England. An affiliation mission sees the strike and the fighter crews get together at the briefing stage and talk through the standard rules of engagement for a sortie of this kind. They will then go off and fly their route to the target, and in turn put up a CAP that intercepts their flightpath at an undisclosed point along the way.

The 'mud movers' will endeavour to evade your interception using ECM or ground hugging techniques, and thus still arrive at their target on track and on time. These missions provide some of the best training available, and nearly all of our overland sorties involve interceptions against Jaguars, Tornado GR.1s, Harrier GR.7s or USAFE aircraft. Individual squadrons from each of the communities will often develop a strong working relationship with each other over a period of time, but this is often difficult to sustain because of other out-of-theatre training commitments.

Flying as the 'number two' in this formation is Batch One Tornado GR.1 ZA473, which was delivered to No 16 Sqn at Laarbruch in June 1984 after spending time in storage at St Athan following its delivery from British Aerospace. Six years later FM was one of a number of No 16 Sqn jets sent to the Gulf, ZA473 donning a shark's mouth and the sobriquet 'Foxy Mama' as part of the Tabuk-based Tornado GR.1 force. FV/ZD812, a Batch Four jet delivered to No 16 Sqn in March 1985, was spared the hardships of a Gulf deployment, remaining in reserve at Laarbruch for the duration of the war

Above A rash of anniversary schemes adorned various aircraft within the GR.1 and F.3 communities in 1990, many of these units celebrating their 75th birthday with garish markings reflecting their individual histories. In my opinion one of the smartest looking paint jobs of the period was the No 16 Sqn effort applied to ZA591. Rather than restrict the scheme to the fin and spine, which many other GR.1 squadrons had done, the unit took the plunge and resprayed the whole airframe satin black, thus reflecting their original day/night Army co-operation role from World War 1. The saint emblem was adopted soon after No 16 Sqn was formed at St Omer, in France, in 1915.

This distinctive looking jet was photographed in-bound to the Spadeadam bombing range in September 1991, just a day or two away from No 16 Sqn's disbandment as part of the Options for Change within RAF Germany. Fellow Laarbruch-based units Nos XV and 20 Sqns were also chopped at the same time. Prior to serving with No 16 Sqn, ZA591 had earlier spent time firstly with No 9 Sqn from February 1982, and then the Tactical Weapons Conversion Unit from October 1986. Besides a pair of inert 1000-lb bombs on the centreline stations, this jet is also equipped with a 'desert pink' ARI.23246/1 Sky Shadow active/passive ECM pod, which functions as a fully autonomous unit when activated

Right Although a GR.1 crew's best form of defence during an affiliation intercept is to stay low, kick in the 'burners and run for cover, the aircraft is often equipped with AIM-9L acquisition rounds, and should you place your mount in a compromising position it will quickly bite back. These No XV Sqn jets were photographed flying over Scarborough in May 1990 as we headed for the North Sea and an affiliation sortie at low-level. Flying in the back seat of the anniversary jet (ZA549) on this occasion was Flt Lt John Nichol who, eight months later, was shot down over Iraq whilst attacking Shaibah air base in ZD791, also a No XV Sqn aircraft. After his repatriation and the eventual disbandment of his former squadron, Flt Lt Nichol was retrained as an F.3 navigator and joined my last Tornado unit, No XI Sqn, in early 1992. The second jet in this photograph, ZA392, was lost on the JP233 strike launched against Shaibah just hours after Flt Lts Nichol and Peters were shot down, pilot Wg Cdr Nigel Elsdon (OC No 27 Sqn) and navigator Flt Lt Max Collier tragically losing their lives in the crash

Above Another strike affiliation favourite with the Leeming squadrons was the recently retired Buccaneer, an aircraft that was almost impossible to stay with once it got its nose down at low-level over the sea. Unfortunately, because of the vast distance between Lossiemouth and our station we rarely flew against them except during exercises. Nos 12 and 208 Sqns tended to fly most of their sorties up over the Moray Firth, restricting their overland missions to a minimum in order to reduce the amount of heavy g-counts their elderly airframes were exposed to. Although few of Lossiemouth's S.2Bs had ever seen a carrier deck, the crews religiously folded the jets' wings as soon as they left the runway, thus preserving one facet of the aircraft's naval ancestry right up to its retirement. Sitting astride an extremely well-weathered S.2B in the winter of 1991, the

navigator of this jet wears a very flash 'No XII Sqn' cloth covering over his bonedome visor. Below him, the aircraft's rotating bomb bay door has been left open for the squadron armourers to perform routine maintenance on the weapon shackles prior to the next flight. Like virtually all other Buccaneers at Lossiemouth at the time, this jet is fitted with an AN/ALQ-101 ECM pod on the starboard outer wing pylon and an AN/AVQ-23E Pave Spike on the port inner station

Above right Besides flying against the Buccaneers, we were occasionally asked to escort them as they practiced their low-level Sea Eagle strike profiles against elements of the Royal Navy. We would arrange over the telephone to meet on the tanker over the North Sea, and from there the mission

commenced. Our briefed profile would see us flying either ahead of or behind the Buccaneers, protecting them by passing on information of the 'enemy' CAP positions and tackling any 'red' F.3s or F-15s/F-16s that tried to engage the strike aircraft. Keeping on course and to the briefed time on target was always a challenge on these flights, as was achieving the intercept at low-level.

XW530 had only recently shed its 'desert pink' scheme when this photograph was taken in late 1991, the jet distinguishing itself as 'Glenmorangie' during a dozen strike missions into Iraq from Muharraq – not a bad effort for an aircraft that celebrated its 21st birthday that same year! Prior to winning its combat spurs with No 12 Sqn, the Buccaneer had earlier spent time with Nos XV, 16, 216 and 208 Sqns. The jet behind it, however, was

even older than XW530, having first been delivered to the Fleet Air Arm as an S.2 on 4 February 1965. XN981 was transferred to the RAF in June 1971, serving firstly with No 237 OCU and then No 12 Sqn, until being given back to the Royal Navy and No 809 Sqn in April 1973.

Converted into a S.2B in the late 1970s, the Buccaneer once again resumed its RAF career when it was issued to No 208 Sqn in April 1979. Fellow Lossiemouth-based unit No 12 Sqn had XN981 on strength in July 1983, before No 208 took it back once again in April 1985! The oldest surviving S.2 in frontline service with the RAF by the early 1990s, it was eventually retired in October 1993 when No 12 Sqn finally stood down with the jet

Above Hunter T.7s and Buccaneer S.2s shared a long and distinguished history at Lossiemouth until both types were declared obsolete and retired in unison. The classic Hawker fighter stood in for the Buccaneer in 1980 when the force was grounded for six months following a fatal fatigue-related crash during a *Red Flag* exercise – the Hunters were used for limited continuation training both at Lossiemouth and Laarbruch whilst the RAF quickly patched up its Buccaneers. A small force were always on strength with No 237 OCU throughout the Buccaneer's service career, the jets being used primarily for navigation and instrument rating training, although the unit's instructors also flew the occasional ACM sortie for the frontline squadrons.

In 1991 two significant events involving the Hunter were celebrated; the type's 40th birthday and the retirement of Air Chief Marshal Sir Patrick Hine. To mark these occasions four

Lossiemouth T.7s were resprayed matt black all over, the scheme reflecting Sir Patrick's previous service with the 'Black Arrows' demonstration team of No 111 Sqn in the late 1950s. A special formation flypast which included these jets, a Lightning F.6, two Phantom FGR.2s and a Harrier T.4, was made over Air Chief Marshal Hine at RAF High Wycombe as a surprise on the day of his retirement.

I was asked to photograph the formation (see next chapter), minus the Lightning, during the morning flypast rehearsal, and whilst most of northern England was covered in low, thick cloud, we cruised around happily snapping away in the warm sunlight at medium altitude. The closest aircraft, XF995, was originally converted to the training role by the Navy, becoming one of three T.8Bs within the Fleet Air Arm. It joined the lead jet (XL568), and two other T.7As, in 1979 when the RAF took charge of all Buccaneer operations in the UK

Above Following two weeks of Tactical Leadership Training at Lossiemouth in Spring 1992, which involved four-ship detachments from various combat squadrons within the RAF, No XI Sqn returned to Leeming accompanied down the east coast by the No 3 Sqn Harrier GR.7 force that had flown in specially from Gütersloh. Leading this formation was an ex-Lightning buddy of mine, Sqn Ldr John Rands, who is currently the 1994 Red Arrows leader. We arranged for an 'Arrows' style line up to take place just prior to the jets breaking off and heading back to Germany, and the 'mud movers' slotted into a slick echelon left formation as briefed when I gave them the signal over the R/T. Affiliation against the GR.5/7 gives you real value for money as they are extremely difficult to track on radar due to their composite structure.

The advanced ECM suite fitted as standard to the aircraft is also highly effective, and the large bubble canopy gives the pilot excellent look-out capabilities at all heights. Although not as fast at low-level as a Tornado GR.1 or Buccaneer S.2B, the GR.5/7's large wing area makes it extremely nimble in trained hands. Each of the GR.7s in this formation are equipped with a finless AIM-9L acquisition round plus a pair of practice bomb dispensers

Phantom II tour

Right For many years a posting to RAF Germany meant weekends away across Europe visiting exotic locations in France, Spain, Italy or even occasionally Greece on two-day 'ranger' flights. A pair of jets would be despatched to a pre-arranged destination last thing on a Friday, and the return trip to Germany would be flown first thing Monday morning. Budgets have shrunk dramatically in the ensuing decade, however, and weekends away are now but a distant memory for the old hands to reminisce about. Having to endure a dose of sunburn underneath my flight suit, I took this photograph of XV497 as we departed the French base of Solenzara, on the island of Corsica, after a most enjoyable 'ranger' in July 1983.

One of the last grey/green FGR.2s with No 19(F) Sqn, this aircraft served the RAF right up until the final Phantom IIs were retired at Wattisham in late 1992, being W within No 74 Sqn. Delivered to the RAF two decades earlier, XV497 was issued to No 41 Sqn at Coningsby in July 1972. Whilst with the unit the jet performed battlefield recce tasks with a belly-mounted EMI pod that boasted a radar, cameras and infrared linescan sensors – only a handful of FGR.2s were modified to carry the drop tank-size pod, and they were operated by either Nos II(AC) or 41 Sqns.

Following a brief spell with No 17 Sqn, which ended in January 1976 when the unit exchanged its FGR.2s for Jaguar GR.1s, the jet became one of the first Phantom IIs issued to No 56 Sqn at Wattisham, replacing the unit's Lightning F.6s. Following an overhaul at St Athan in the early 1980s, XV497 was issued to No 19(F) Sqn in 1982, the aircraft staying at Wildenrath for over five years until being sent to the Falklands as 'Desperation' for No 1435 Flight. It returned to Wattisham and was briefly placed in storage in 1990, before being issued to No 74 Sqn in January 1991 when the unit retired its F-4J(UK)s

Left and above Being in the right place at the right time again allowed me to photograph the one-off all-blue No 92 Sqn disbandment aircraft, which temporarily joined the ranks of No 56 Sqn following the closure of Wildenrath in early 1992. The aircraft had flown up to Leeming for the base open day, and we had accompanied the FGR.2 back to Wattisham on the Monday as No XI Sqn had requested a session of DACT with No 56 Sqn prior to the Firebirds' disbandment. Although No 92 Sqn had flown their last Phantom II sortie almost a year before this photograph was taken in June 1992, XV408 was retained in airworthy condition primarily so that it could attend a handful of RAF open days before being finally grounded in the autumn. By this stage the scheme, which had also been applied to No 19(F) Sqn's XT899, was beginning to weather, and a non-blue undercarriage door had had to be fitted at Wattisham in place of the damaged original article. The aircraft is also carrying a tatty looking baggage pod and an AIM-9L acquisition round. The crew for this flight were Flt Lt Rick Offord, who is now flying F/A-18s with the Royal Australian Air Force, and Sqn Ldr Jack Christen, who is currently serving as OC of a Bulldog-equipped UAS. During its 22 years in the RAF, XV408 spent time with Nos 6, 23, 19(F) and 92 Sqns, as well as with No 228 OCU

Above The pilot of a No 56 Sqn jet uses hand signals to communicate with his groundcrew as the FGR.2 fires up on the ramp at Brawdy during a JMC exercise in 1990. When I was a navigator with No 19(F) Sqn I would assist the pilot in a variety of ways both before and during a typical ACT sortie. This would usually start with me obtaining the briefing slides prior to the actual brief taking place, and booking the airspace, which was crucial in Germany because there wasn't really much of it. ACT could in those days be performed down to 500 and up to 24,000 ft, but it had to be over an unpopulated area like the Ardennes Forest. I also had to get in touch with the GCI operators and inform them of what we wanted to achieve from the sortie. As a navigator, you would tell them details like 'this is going to be a one v one sortie and the first call sign will be Mike Lima Five One. Our opponent is the target and we are the fighter.'

I would also inform them of what type of threat our opponent was simulating, be it a *Flogger Bravo, Fishbed* or *Fitter*, what weapons we were simulating, and most importantly what the kill criterion was. This could perhaps take the form of a 25-mile split, and then prior to the merge there would be no kills, thus ensuring a close in visual fight – this allowed you to partake in some serious 'doggers'! Further mission criterion like no kills ahead of the '3/9 line' (stern quarter), or one valid 'heater' (AIM-9G/L) and a gun shot would result in a confirmed victory, were also laid down.

We would crew up as the sorties dictated, and I had no dedicated pilot exclusively to myself during the tour. Young navigators tended to team up with experienced pilots, and vice versa. The missions flown in the Tornado F.3 are far more complex than those attempted ten years ago in the FGR.2 primarily because the RAF of the 1990s is a more capable force than it was then. Packages of aircraft, supported closely by both tankers and fighters can be flown on far ranging sorties as and when tasked. The scenarios have also become more complex, a crew maybe dealing with air combat, air-to-ground, ECM and flight refuelling all in the one sortie. This has primarily come about because of the diversification of the threat, which has now moved from Europe to virtually a global stage

Above right The full formation for the retirement flypast of Air Marshal Sir Patrick Hine, bar the Lightning, which came down from Warton. England was blanketed with low cloud on the day of the rehearsal, so the five-ship, plus my photo-Hawk, climbed through it after departing Brize Norton and cruised around at height running through the various formation positions prior to the full flypast being flown in the afternoon. The closest FGR.2 had actually been issued to the A&AEE at Boscombe Down following its acceptance by the RAF for radio trials work. Its first spell with No 56 Sqn occured in the mid 1970s, during which time it was damaged in an accident. Repaired and returned to service, it was transferred to No 228 OCU in 1982, then passed on to No 23 Sqn in January 1983, and then back to the 'Firebirds' just two months later. There it stayed until it was scrapped at Wattisham in September 1992

Right Flt Lt Rick Offord shows off his flying skills in a conventionally painted No 56 Sqn jet as our small formation heads from Leeming to Warton for a low-level affiliation sortie against the 'Firebirds' over the Pennines. The FGR.2 in this essentially clean configuration, bar a single wing-mounted AIM-9L acquisition round and two finless SkyFlash in the forward fuselage troughs, was a fair match for the F.3 in a tight DACT fight, the jet's large wing area giving the unencumbered Phantom II a healthy rate of turn. The FGR.2's twin Rolls-Royce Spey Mk 202 turbofans worked at their best during ACM performed at altitudes above 20,000 ft, whereas the F.3 had the ascendancy at heights of around 5000 ft. Therefore, the FGR.2 crews would attempt to drag us up to their favoured altitude and we would fight to bring them down to ours!

Opposite To commemorate the disbandment of the 'Firebirds' on 1 July 1992, I was asked to photograph the last big unit push with the Phantom II that was flown early the month before. The squadron's ability to get nine well-used FGR.2s up into the same patch of sky for this photo-sortie spoke volumes about the professionalism of No 56 Sqn's maintenance section. Whilst XV470/D and XV472/A held out of shot, the remaining seven jets fell into line astern behind XV426/P, the resulting formation proving once and for all that fast jet pilots can spell as well as fly, and occasionally do both at the same time. Following a couple of minutes in this position whilst I shot off several rolls of Fuji RVP from my Hawk camera platform, the jets were rejoined by the missing pair and a classic diamond nine formation carefully evolved in front of my lens. Marked up with a large squadron badge on the fin and flown by the head 'Firebird', XV470 slotted into the lead position, with XV472 flying off his starboard wing.

This allowed the new formation to be accurately assembled with minimal positional changes from the earlier phoenix line up

Above When we launched on this sortie out of Wattisham the weather at the Suffolk base was dreadful, but luckily the Met Office had informed us of clearer skies off the coast so we headed north east across the North Sea. Sure enough, the visibility improved the further we flew away from the station and we eventually settled on a clear patch of sky for unlimited formation work. Although the fuselages of the FGR.2s looked relatively clean, once the aircraft were viewed in planform the true state of the squadron's weary mounts became plainly obvious. Streaked with fluid and scuffed by the groundcrews' black-soled boots, the wing area of each of the jets exhibited signs of heavy use by the 'Firebirds', who flew a full programme of exercises right up until their 'undeclaration' to NATO

Right The Queen's official birthday flypast is performed on 16 June every year, the formation enjoying that rare privilege of cruising over central London at a moderately low altitude as they line up for their run over Buckingham Palace. In 1993 the formation was made up of soon to be retired Buccaneers and Victors, whilst the year before the honour had fallen to the Wattisham wing. Leading a Balbo of 16 aircraft comprising an even nunber of jets from Nos 56 and 74 Sqns, AVM John Allison did the honours at the helm of XV474, the flagship of the Tiger Squadron.

   The formation was carefully arranged in four boxes of four jets, the outer flanks of the Balbo consisting of No 56 Sqn jets whilst the No 74 Sqn Phantom IIs formed the forward and aft portions of the group – visually impressive, the Balbo requires high levels of concentration and deft flying skill to be exhibited by all 32 aircrew involved. It is also a difficult event to photograph as the camera-ship has to be some distance away from the Balbo to fit all 16 jets in! I had to compromise when I took this shot and crop the trailing No 74 Sqn jet out of the photograph – sorry guys! This formation flew up to Coningsby immediately after the flypast, participating in the station's open day, before recovery back at Wattisham. Adorned with an oversize tiger's head on its fin, XV474 had transferred in from No 56 Sqn once No 74 had retired its F-4J(UK)s. Its unique serial made the jet a natural candidate for the coveted position of OC's mount, and it duly became T, replacing XV393. Prior to this the aircraft had served with Nos 17, II(AC), 56, 29 (in the Falklands) and 23 Sqns, and was thus an ideal candidate for preservation at Imperial War Museum Duxford, where it now resides

Above One jet that didn't escape the cutter's torch, however, was XV487, which was disposed of at Wattisham in late 1992 following No 74 Sqn's disbandment on 1 October that year. We flew many DACT sorties against the FGR.2s in 1992 as the units attempted to use up the remaining airframe hours on the well-worn jets – this particular shot was taken after a one v one trip against Sqn Ldr Dom Reilly (ex-Red Arrows), a former Wildenrath mate from my No 19(F) Sqn days, and that year's display navigator, Flt Lt Mark Mainwaring, who is modelling his smart airshow bonedome. The FGR.2 was a good BVR-capable target for the F.3 because it exhibited vastly different operational characteristics to the Tornado. This particular jet spent several years being rebuilt in the mid-1970s following a CAT.3 engine fire in February 1973 at Brüggen

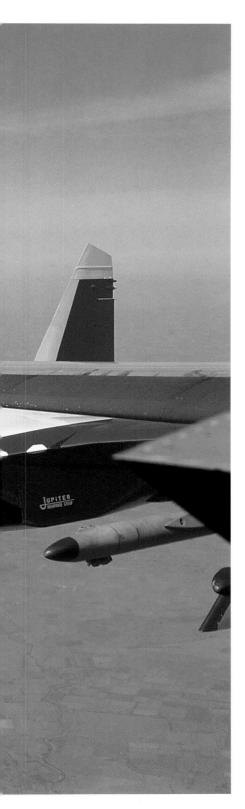

European connection

Left In June 1992 the first civil Su-27 flew across from Russia to perform at a handful of displays in the UK. Two *Flankers* were originally scheduled to attend the International Air Tattoo (IAT) at Boscombe Down on June 13/14, and I arranged with the event organisers to intercept the Russians out over the channel and escort them back to Hampshire. This was viewed as a good training sortie for us, and quite by chance No XI Sqn was contributing an F.3 for the IAT static line in any case, leaving the other jet parked on the 'live' side of the airfield. Strike Command gave us approval and the IAT gave me a telephone number for the Gromov Flight Research Centre, who flew the Su-27s from the experimental airfield at Zhukovsky. Only a year before I had been intercepting *Bears* over the North Sea and now here I was phoning Moscow direct from the No XI Sqn crewroom at Leeming, speaking with the navigator for the flight about where he was planning to enter UK airspace! He spoke reasonable English and we eventually decided to rendezvous off the coast of Clacton as that was about the only place that he knew.

All these arrangements were originally scheduled to take place on Thursday or Friday, but because of overflight problems with some of the newly independent states that now border Russia, the aircraft didn't depart until Saturday. We launched at 1400 but once airborne we realised that the time they had given us was an hour later than we had briefed here in the UK, so we had to land at Mildenhall and refuel on route! After a rapid turnaround, we launched and immediately climbed to 30,000 ft, where we finally intercepted Anatoly Kvotchur in the Su-27P and his support crew in an Aeroflot Tu-134A. The legendary Russian test pilot immediately slotted in close under my starboard wing, and we could clearly see how large an aircraft the *Flanker* really was, and how far back the pilot sat from the radome. The aircraft's finish was clearly not up to Western standards, but its manoeuvrability was, as Anatoly ably demonstrated for me with a couple of quick snap rolls.

We cruised across to Boscombe Down, where the ATC told us to hold whilst *La Patrouille de France* finished their routine. I asked the Russians if they could delay their recovery after their long flight from Zhukhovsky, and Anatoly replied through his navigator/interpreter in the Tu-134 that he still had an hour's fuel left and he wanted to perform an impromptu display prior to landing. This was a clear indication of the huge range the *Flanker* possessed on internal fuel only. Afterwards, I met Kvotchur in the hospitality area and my lasting memory was that his handshake was similar to that of a tractor driver's! He kept telling me about how he had watched with some amazement the continual movement of the manoeuvre flaps on my F.3 whilst we were in close formation – these devices are rarely seen on Russian combat aircraft

Above The commercially-sponsored *Flankers* of the 'Test Pilots' team have been stunning additions to the UK airshow scene over the past two years, and their mount, the single-seat Su-27P, is a dedicated interceptor version based on the more common *Flanker-B*. These aircraft were the first P/PU models built by Sukhoi, and as such lack most of the military avionics fitted to the production-standard aircraft. They are owned by the Jupiter Insurance Group, hence their unusual 'house colours' scheme which is based on the 'new' Russian flag. The Aeroflot Tu-134A has been exclusively used to support the *Flankers* during their forays across to the UK, the airliner normally being employed by the LII test establishment at Zhukovsky on transport and liaison duties

Right In September 1991 the newly formed Russian Knights aerobatic demonstration team visited the Red Arrows at Scampton on their first overseas goodwill visit from their base at Kubinka. The 'Arrows' asked No 29 Sqn to intercept the team when they entered UK airspace because the F.3 was radar-equipped, so a four-ship was despatched from Coningsby and they duly escorted the six Su-27s back to Scampton. The four F.3s chosen to perform this historic flight were all fitted with external tanks as No 29 Sqn was scheduled to deploy to Cyprus for an APC the following day. I tagged along in a Hawk to record the event on film, and luckily we came across a patch of blue sky just as the full ten-ship formation banked on a course change, this manoeuvre being performed as if all the aircraft were joined as one

Right I closed in on the *Flankers* after taking the group shot and photographed some of the aircraft individually within the formation. Although these jets all wore the elaborate Russian Knights scheme, which incorporated a VVS (Air Forces) flag on the aircrafts' tailfins, each Su-27 was still fully combat capable, a fact denoted by the missile pylons under the wings and fuselage. The team hailed from the 234th 'Proskurovskii' Guards Fighter Regiment, and was equipped with production standard Su-27 *Flanker-B* single-seaters and Su-27UB *Flanker-C* twins. The 'Proskurovskii' Guards control several squadrons at Kubinka, all of which operate primarily as demonstration and display units

Above This unique formation was photographed transiting from Fairford to Chivenor in July 1991 following the Tiger Meet at the Wiltshire base which had seen participation from the Czech Air Force for the very first time. A pair of MiG-29s from the Zatec-based No 1 Sqn, part of No 1 Wing, deployed to the UK along with a single MiG-23ML, two L-39s, a Tu-134 and an An-12. When the MiGs departed Fairford on the Tuesday and headed west for Chivenor's Open Day, a pair of Hawk T.1As from No 2 TWU escorted them throughout the short flight. As can be seen from this shot the Czech pilots maintained a rigid formation with the Sidewinder-armed Hawk for the full duration of the flight, the MiG-23 filling the trail slot a short distance behind.

Both *Fulcrum-A*s were heavily 'zapped' whilst at Fairford, and the Czechs efforts at 'tiger striping' the fins of their aircraft were much appreciated by the event's organisers and enthusiasts alike. The aircraft closest to the camera was suffering from an unspecified problem with its starboard Klimov RD.33 turbofan throughout the flight, the pilot choosing to open the overwing intakes to ensure that the engine wasn't starved of airflow at any point during the short sortie. Although 40 *Fulcrum-A*s were originally ordered by the then communist government of Czechoslovakia in the late 1980s, only 12 were delivered following a decision to halt military spending in 1990 by the newly elected democratic parliament due to economic pressures. Now that the nation has split into the Czech Republic and Slovakia, all of the MiG-29s are operated from Zatec by the former country

Above Just as all the *Fulcrum-A*s have been absorbed into the 'new' Czech Air Force, so too have most of the 250+ MiG-23s flown by the air arm since the late 1970s. Four separate marks of *Flogger* were bought at bargain basement prices (reportedly $6.6 each) from Mikoyan, the largest order being for the strike-optimised MiG-23BN *Flogger-H* (140), which were issued to the 28th Fighter Bomber Regiment at Caslav in 1979. 105 MiG-23MG *Flogger-B* fighters had been delivered to the 1st Fighter Regiment the year before, the unit being based at Ceske Budejovice. This particular jet was part of a batch of 45 MiG-23ML *Flogger-G* attrition replacements received in 1985 and issued to the fighter regiment. The ML derivative of *Flogger-G* is lighter than the MF and benefits from upgraded avionics, improved aerodynamics and the installation of the uprated Khatchatourov R-35-300 turbojet engine.

Having two generations of MiG together allowed me to compare the two types on the wing quite closely. The lack of visibility for the pilot in the *Flogger-B* was plainly obvious, as was its lack of manoeuvrability even in this undemanding environment – the wings were never swept throughout the flight, and when it turned it did so with rigid, angular movements. The prominent devil motif on the nose of the aircraft is the unit insignia for the 1st Fighter Regiment

Right In comparison to the MiG-23ML, the seamless contouring of the F-16A makes the former General Dynamics, now Lockheed, fighter appear to be from the 21st century. In reality, this Fighting Falcon actually flew for the first time from Fokker's Schipol plant several years before the *Flogger-G* was built by Mikoyan! Taking advantage of the 'dug in' HASs at Andøya, I scrambled atop one of these structures to photograph this No 338 Skv F-16A as it taxied out for a combined CAP sortie with a No XI Sqn Tornado F.3 during joint exercises in 1992. The hours of windtunnel testing put in by GD's design team, led by Harry J Hillaker, resulted in the revolutionary blended wing-body concept which gave the jet outstanding levels of lift at high angles of attack. The unobstructed visibility enjoyed by the pilot can also be appreciated from this elevated vantage point

Above The Norwegians are very professional F-16 operators, performing all manner of tasks with their aircraft ranging from pure air defence, to ground attack and anti-shipping strikes – No 338 Skv share the latter responsibility with Bodø-based No 334 Skv, the units' primary weapon being the indigenous Kongsberg Penguin Mk3. During the height of the Cold War, these two units would have been charged with the key responsibility of sinking Soviet warships as they attempted to break out from Murmansk through the Norwegian Sea into the Atlantic. However, on today's sortie all of the pilots in these F-16s have their minds set firmly in air defence mode, the Tactical Fighter Meet exercise pitting No XI Sqn and elements of No 338 Skv against other RNAF elements tasked with 'taking out' Andøya. It was a real feat of engineering to get the massed ranks of defenders and attackers airborne at the same time from several bases during the morning and afternoon missions – 20+ jets launching and recovering in quick succession was an awe-inspiring sight

Left A total of 72 Fighting Falcons were delivered to the Royal Norwegian Air Force (RNAF) between January 1980 and June 1984 – six attrition replacements were delivered some years later. Of this number, 14 were two-seat F-16Bs, six of which are operated by the Fighting Falcon OCU, No 322 Skv, at Rygge. However, each of the three frontline units usually contain at least a single B-model within their ranks, and in 1992 80-3689 was one of a pair assigned to Ørland-based No 338 Skv. A clear indication of the jet's previous posting is visible forward of the sooty cannon port, the faded grey lightning bolt having originally been applied in dark blue by No 331 Skv at Bodø some years earlier.

Most European F-16 operators tend to fly their aircraft equipped with AIM-9s on both wingtip pylons on all sorties, as pilots believe that the fully-finned dummy rounds give the jet just that little bit extra manoeuvrability particularly at high altitude. The pilot of this F-16B is obviously convinced of their worth as he has an AIM-9J on both wingtips, plus a pylon mounted AIM-9L – the dayglo colouring of the port round is also used as a recognition aid by 'friendly' crews whilst performing low-level CAPs against 'enemy' F-16s

Above This atmospheric shot was taken following our mission debrief at Bodø after the successful completion of the large 'mud package' strike on Andøya. On the return trip to our island base I was guided through Vestfjorden by a highly seasoned F-16 pilot who flew with the call sign of 'Jimmy Red'! Due to the general lack of pollution in this part of the world, Norway enjoys some of the most stunning sunsets in Europe – perfect for framing an F-16 against

Left Having successfully defended the island base of Andøya yet again, a No XI Sqn F.3 flown by Sqn Ldr Chris Taylor, formates with an F-16A of No 338 Skv up from Ørland. The pilot of the Fighting Falcon is Flt Lt Steve Coombs, an RAF exchange officer enjoying a three-year posting with the squadron. The Norwegians are highly respected for their prowess with the F-16, and some of the flying that they do, like night close formation take-offs and low-level interceptions down the fjords, raise the hairs on the back of an RAF fast jet pilot's neck! The topography in this part of the world is hugely impressive, and the RNoAF crews' knowledge of each and every fjord in their 'patch' is equally amazing. Pilots spend hours learning the height and length of each rock face, as well as the exact position of high-tension electricity cables which stretch across the country from fjord to fjord. Flying above us at high altitude during this sortie were a pair of Russian I1-38 ELINT aircraft, kept at a suitable distance away from the exercise area by the RNoAF's QRA F-16s

Above Soon after completing my deployment to Andøya I was despatched to Scandinavia once again to participate in a NATO-run Tactical Fighter Weapons course for F-16s that was being held at Skrydstrup in Denmark. All four Fighting Falcon operators in Western Europe send aircraft to these courses, and I hoped to fly against a formation that included an example from each participating air force. Things weren't looking promising on the afternoon I had arranged for the photography to take place as the Norwegians had failed to generate a single sortie all morning through technical glitches afflicting their pair of F-16s. However, when we finally launched and formed up, the Dutch F-16 was conspicuous by its absence, so I had to make do with a second Danish Fighting Falcon instead.

No XI Sqn had been invited to Denmark because of our BVR capability, and a typical sortie would see a pair of F.3s up against a quartet of F-16s, one from each of the nations participating. We acquitted ourselves well in this environment

because we utilised the jets' BVR capabilities at all times, thus avoiding the turning fight, where we knew all too well from our past experiences that the Fighting Falcon was more than a handful for the F.3. To counter our SkyFlash lock the F-16 pilots would manipulate their RWR equipment in an attempt to gain valuable miles in the battle to the merge. Flying as a fighting pair, my wingman and I briefed beforehand how close we would allow the F-16s to approach before we broke off the fight

Right On the sortie that this photograph was taken I operated as a singleton against a pair of F-16As from the then recently formed No 314 Sqn, Royal Netherlands Air Force, and a single Fighting Falcon from 349 Smaldeel/1 Wing of the Belgian Air Force. Both the Dutch jets carried dummy AIM-9Js on the port wing pylons and AIM-9L acquisition rounds on the starboard rail, whilst the Belgian F-16 was restricted to a seeker round on the port wing pylon only. In a 'shooting war' it is highly unlikely

that a single F.3 would launch itself into combat against three enemy aircraft, but when you're on det at the invitation of your NATO brethren sacrifices have to be made. No XI Sqn became involved in small two-ship deployments to Scandinavia after an enjoyable squadron exchange with Eskadrille 726 at Aalborg. Our reputation for filling the BVR slot at short notice quickly spread through the 'old boy network', and if our operational schedule allowed, my squadron boss was keen to accommodate any reasonable request for F.3 participation. The chance to fly against other NATO types in DACT missions is always a great boon for Tornado F.3 crews as the opportunity to perform similar sorties in the UK is restricted to dissimilar air combat missions with TWU Hawk T.1As.

These dets usually last for two days only and no groundcrew are taken. In that time you will usually fly five or six sorties, performing an aircrew turnaround at the end of every flight. This procedure sees the pilot and navigator checking the oil levels and the engine gearbox prior to the next launch. It makes for a long day after a serious session of ACM, but conversely it gives you a greater empathy with the F.3's systems and mechanical foibles. To facilitate the minimal servicing carried out the jet whilst away, a small tool kit is given to the aircrew prior to departure from their home station. Turnaround training is undertaken once a year by both the pilot and navigator under the supervision of the groundcrew, a currency certificate being awarded upon the successful completion of this day-long exercise

Above Due to their joint TFW training, most Western NATO F-16 drivers tackle the BVR threat in a similar way, using the jet's Dalmo Victor AN/ALR-69 RWR equipment (or the Loral Rapport III system, housed in the extended tail compartment in place of a parachute in the Belgian jets) to counter the F.3's Foxhunter radar. Pilots of the two Dutch units at Leeuwarden, Nos 322 and 323 Sqns, are amongst the hardest to counter in BVR scenarios as they have spent many years training against the USAFE's 32nd Fighter Squadron with their F-15Cs at nearby Soesterberg – the Eagles left Holland for good in late 1993, thus eliminating another source of DACT training. The Danes are also effective operators, and the healthy squadron exchange programme they have established with the F.3 community has meant that both air forces have mutually benefitted from comparing different ways of countering the aerial threat. This F-16A from Eskadrille 730 was photographed in July 1990 during the unit's visit to Leeming, where they were hosted by No 25(F) Sqn. Coded 'E-174', this veteran jet was in fact the very first single-seat Fighting Falcon delivered to the Danes from the SABCA/Avions Fairey plant in Belgium way back in January 1980 – this airframe was followed by a further 53 A- and 16 B-models

Left Talking of 'twin-stick' F-16s, this is the view from the back seat – I took this self-portrait as the jet skimmed over the water off the coast of Skrydstrup on an anti-shipping strike during a reciprocal exchange with Eskadrille 730 in the spring of 1990. Although this frontline unit only had a single F-16B on strength at the time, several aircraft were 'borrowed' from fellow-ramp mates Eskadrille 727 who operate as the Danish OCU for the Fighting Falcon. This sortie gave me a valuable insight into the jet's capabilities as an opponent as I got to examine its Westinghouse APG-66 radar at close quarters, and see the high workload the pilot has to endure at critical phases in the flight. I first saw an F-16 in 1976 when I cycled from school to Bentwaters to watch a prototype YF-16 take on a USAFE F-4E soon after the jet had dazzled the crowds at that year's Farnborough. During the brief flight the Phantom II pilot forlornly flew a procession of max rate turns as he tried to get on the tail of the nimble jet, which was circling effortlessly within the circumference of the F-4E's ragged manoeuvres

Above One nation that didn't buy F-16s in the late 1970s is Italy, its Aeronautica Militare Italiana (AMI) deciding instead to purchase more F-104 Starfighters (it received its last new-build F-104S as late as 1979) to fulfil both the interceptor and strike roles. Now, as the Italian government awaits the outcome of the European Fighter Aircraft (EFA) debate, the backbone of its air force is looking at having to soldier on into the 21st century with the last 'century series' fighters in Europe! In 1993 a rare squadron exchange took place between the RAF and the AMI, 4° Stormo/9° Gruppo sending eight Starfighters from Grossetto to Leeming where they were hosted by No XI Sqn. I had flown against the F-104 on many occasions in the early 1980s during my Phantom II days, but I had never photographed the jet on the wing before.

On this particular sortie the Italians coaxed four jets skyward for a four v four fight against our F.3s, but the F-104's poor turning circle, allied with its tell-tale smoke trail left behind by its rasping General Electric J79 turbojet, meant that the Starfighter was no match for a competent Tornado crew. In the back of the TF-104G on this trip was my old squadron boss, Wg Cdr Cliffe, who had previously flown Lightnings. He described the cockpit of a Starfighter as being smelly, dirty and noisy – just like a Lightning!

Above On 16 November 1993 the relevance of the squadron exchange that had taken place earlier in the year became plainly obvious as Italian defence minister Fabio Fabbri announced that 24 surplus RAF Tornado F.3s were to be leased by the AMI for a ten-year period as stop-gap fighters, pending the introduction of the Eurofighter 2000 into service. Interested parties within the AMI had been pushing for the F.3's acquisition since as early as 1988, and as the EFA programme continued to slip further sideways it became obvious that something had to be done. A number of proposals were studied including the purchase of surplus F-15s and F-16s, but the F.3's spares and training commonality with the AMI's large Tornado IDS force eventually swayed the deal in favour of the RAF interceptor.

The two units tipped to receive the aircraft in place of their F-104S/ASA Starfighters are 36° Stormo/12° Gruppo at Gioia del Colle, near Bari, and 37° Stormo/18° Gruppo at Trapani, on the island of Sicily. The remaining five Gruppo will share the 80 to 90 late-build Starfighters chosen for upgrading to F-104 ASA/M specs, which will see some re-winging carried out, engines upgraded and new electronics and avionics fitted

Left Two years prior to the Starfighter visit, I was fortunate enough to spend a fortnight in Spain with No XI Sqn during a unit exchange with Escadron 151, part of Ala 15, at Zaragoza near Barcelona. This was a rare treat for us as the unit's EF-18As were all BVR capable, with their AIM-7 Sparrows linked into the jet's awesome Hughes APG-65 radar. Slick operators with a solid handle on the Hornet's capabilities, the Spanish impressed us with the complex sorties they generated which involved multi-bogey intercepts against a variety of dissimilar adversaries including Mirage IIIEs and Mirage F1CEs and EEs. We also flew either with the EF-18s on our side against these types, or against them as they attacked us in mixed formations.

All the Spanish Hornets looked as well-used as this EF-18B, including the one I was strapped into when I took this photograph – my pilot on this occasion was a Captain Alonso. I was impressed by the Hornet's CRT displays during my orientation flight, although I thought the jet's instantaneous turn and roll rate was inferior to the F-16. The aircraft was very noisy and prone to buffeting whilst being manoeuvred in this fashion, and in this respect it reminded me a lot of the Lightning

Above In December 1992 we got an unusual request from the 77th TFS at Upper Heyford for some fighter affiliation training against their F-111Es. In the 22 years that the 20th TFW had flown out of its base in Oxfordshire, few pure ACT sorties had ever been generated against RAF assets, the 'mud movers' preferring to use their speed and low-level agility to keep out of the fighters' way. I jumped at the chance to 'hassle' with these soon to be retired 'Cold War' warriors, never having flown against them in this way before.

Equipped with rather dated AIM-9P acquisition rounds on the starboard pylons, and toting an AN/ALQ-101 ECM pod under the rear fuselage, the F-111E was a gallant, yet hopelessly outclassed opponent on this fine winter's day. Although the crews used the Doppler capability of their General Electric APC-113 radar to good effect, acquiring us at a considerable distance, we also picked them up early primarily because of their size. Similarly, their lack of ACM currency meant they fought a very flat fight, the vertical plain being avoided at all times. As the hard deck for the sortie was 5000 ft, they couldn't stick their noses down and run away. I had only previously worked with F-111s during low-level intercept evasion training, where their impressive acceleration often came into play

Above The 140+ F-111E/Fs that provided the backbone around which the USAFE strike force was built for over 20 years have been totally replaced now by just two squadrons operating a total of 48 F-15E Strike Eagles out of Lakenheath, in Suffolk. The 492nd and 494th Fighter Squadrons form the 48th Fighter Wing, which of course was previously the 48th TFW, who's three F-111F units wreaked havoc when finally unleashed against an unexpected enemy in the form of Iraq in January/February 1991. It is unlikely that a force of barely four-dozen F-15Es could be as effective as 150 F-111s, but times have changed, both politically and technologically, and the state-of-the-art avionics embodied in the Strike Eagle make it a true multi-role combat aircraft. I flew a handful of affiliation sorties with the F-15E prior to my leaving No XI Sqn, but at this point in their Strike Eagle re-equipment programme the crews were still coming to terms with their aircrafts' seemingly boundless capabilities. Both these aircraft were intercepted heading for the bombing ranges in Northumberland, their only offensive stores being a single SUU-20 practice bomb/rocket launcher, with six 25-lb blue bombs per dispenser, under each wing

Above As this book goes to press in the Spring of 1994 I am currently 'part of' the *Armée de l'Air*, or 5° Escadre de Chasse to be more specific. As an air defence pilot, 'exchange' postings are limited to other nations' fighter/air defence aircraft. Currently, the RAF has pilots flying exchange on F-15s in the USA, F/A-18s in Australia, F-16s in Norway and F-4Fs in Germany. The latest 'exchange' posting is with the French at Orange, in the south of the country, flying the Mirage 2000C – originally, the post was at Colmar on the venerable Mirage III. With the almost simultaneous introduction of the Tornado F.3 and the Mirage 2000 on either side of the Channel, the two air forces set up an 'exchange' – my French counterpart is currently flying F.3s with No 29 Sqn at Coningsby.

My reasons for bidding for the French post stemmed largely from a visit I made to Orange in May 1989. I was immediately impressed by the aircraft's handling qualities, its single-seat attributes and of course the 'provencal' lifestyle and climate. One of the stipulations of the job, however, was a fluency in French, so for most of 1993 I was firmly grounded at Waterbeach barracks, in Cambridgeshire, learning to speak the language. However, by the time I arrived in France in September 1993, I was able to start my new vocation with some degree of fluency.

By coincidence, over 12 months before moving to Orange, my first opportunity to photograph Mirage 2000s saw me shooting jets from Escadron de Chasse 1/5 'Vendée', one of three units within 5° Escadre de Chasse – the jets from 1° Escadrille had deployed to Leeming in May 1992 as part of Orange's then reciprocal exchange programme with No 23 Sqn

Above On this particular flight a mixed mission profile involving two Hawk T.1As, two Mirage 2000s and a pair of F.3s was flown out over the North Sea. The French pilots knew the capabilities of their aircraft extremely well, fighting almost exclusively at heights between 30,000 and 40,000 ft where the jet's SNECMA M53 turbofan engine performed at its best. Its ability to cruise around all day at this altitude was one of the things that instantly appealed to me about the Mirage 2000, most of my flying since the demise of the Lightning F.6 having been performed at heights between 15,000 to 30,000 ft. The aircraft's cockpit is also a snug fit for an average size pilot, just like the old Lightning. The ability to cruise at 0.9 Mach all day was also a major draw, a feature which I had again not experienced for an awfully long time

Right The *Desert Storm* (codenamed *Opération Salamandre*) campaign saw EC5 fly over 1400 sorties during their eight-month stay at Al Ahsa, and although photographed a year after its Saudi excursion had ended, this Mirage 2000B of 2° Escadrille was still fitted with sand-coloured missile pylons when despatched to Leeming in May 1992. A finless MATRA 550 Magic 2 acquisition round is carried on the jet's port outer pylon, this infrared homing short-range weapon having been developed from the Magic 1, which initially entered service in 1975. The latter version is basically similar to the AIM-9L in terms of its capabilities, although the seeker head, made by SAT, can function either independently of the Mirage's RDI radar, or in a slaved manner responding to the system's guidance instructions.

The Mirage 2000B itself is identical to the 2000C, the 'twin' lacking only the cannon and about five minutes fuel. On arrival at EC 2/2 – the fighter OCU at Dijon – I soon discovered why the Mirage 2000 display pilot always uses the two-seat variety for his routine. Unlike F.3 aircrew, who perform rudimentary servicing on their jets whilst on deployment, all pre- and post-flight maintenance on the Mirage 2000 is carried out by qualified engineers, hence the need for the second seat. I assume the 'passenger' becomes a spectator during the display itself, as 'sandbagging' during a 9g low-level display sequence is not for the faint-hearted!

Above During my three-year Mirage 2000 tour I should accrue a total of 600 hours on type, and like F.3 postings, where a lot of time is spent flying away from home, detachments to Italy and Saudi Arabia are a certainty. A limited ground attack tasking is also performed by all Mirage 2000C units, and this is a phase of operational flying that I haven't performed since my Brawdy days in 1985! The Orange wing is responsible for undertaking deployments to the Middle East in support of French forces, either operating independently or in conjunction with UN partners

Specifications

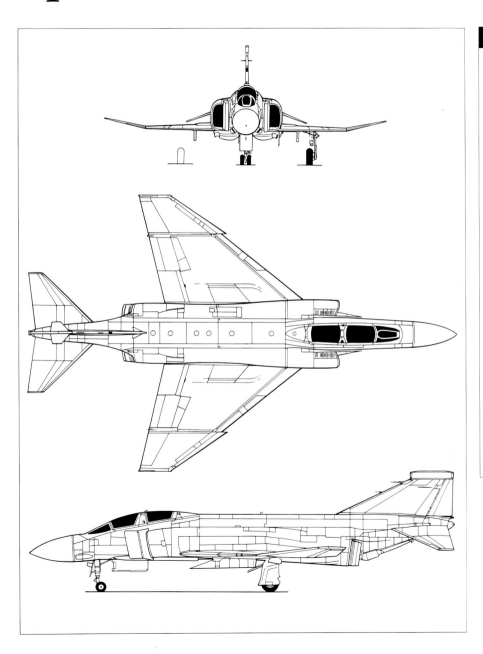

McDonnell Douglas Phantom FGR.2

Flown from February 1981 to February 1984 during my first operational tour as a navigator with No 19(F) Sqn at RAFG Wildenrath

Type: all-weather multi-role fighter for land operation

Engines: two 20,515 lb (9305 kg) Rolls-Royce Spey 202/203 two-shaft augmented turbofans

Dimensions: span 38 ft 5 in (11.7 m); length 57 ft 7 in (17.55 m); height 16 ft 3 in (4.96 m)

Weights: 31,000 lb (14,060 kg); maximum loaded 58,000 lb (26,308 kg)

Performance: maximum speed with SkyFlash missiles only (low) 920 mph, (high) 1386 mph; initial climb, typically 32,000 ft/min; service ceiling, over 60,000 ft: range on internal fuel (no weapons) about 1750 miles (2817 km); ferry range with external fuel, typically 2300 miles (3700 km)

Armament: four SkyFlash air-to-air missiles recessed under fuselage; inner wing pylons can carry two more SkyFlash or four AIM-9 Sidewinder missiles; in addition a multi-barrel 20 mm gun could be carried externally in a centreline pod; four wing pylons for tanks, bombs or other stores to total weight of 16,000 lbs (7257 kg)

History: first flight (XF4H-1) 27 May 1958; YF-4K (FG.1) 27 June 1966

English Lightning

Flown from September 1986 until June 1988, firstly with the Lightning Training Flight and then No XI Sqn, both at RAF Binbrook, Lincolnshire

Powerplant: two Rolls-Royce Avon 302-C turbojet engines (each 16,300 lb; 7393 kg st with afterburning)

Wing span: 34 ft 10 in (10.61 m)

Length overall: 55 ft 3 in (16.84 m), including probe

Max take-off weight: approx 48,000 lb (21,770 kg)

Max level speed at operational height: above 1146 kts (1320 mph; 2124 km/h)

Armament: two 30 mm Aden guns can be carried. Weapon bay could accommodate one of a variety of operational packs. These included a twin-Firestreak or twin-Red Top air-to-air missile pack, or a rocket pack with two retractable launchers for a total of 44 x 2 in spin-stabilised rockets. Two pylons beneath outer wings, each capable of carrying two 1000-lb HE, retarded or fire bombs, two Matra 155 launchers for 18 WNEB 68 mm rockets apiece, two flare pods or two machine-gun pods

Variants:

F.3/3A: Rolls-Royce Avon 301, air-to-air missile armament only, and larger square-topped tail fin. Reduced outer-wing sweep on F.3A. Most converted later to F.6

T.4: side-by-side two-seat unarmed trainer

T.5: side-by-side two-seat trainer; Avon 301 engines, provision for missiles

F.6: Last production version for RAF; Avon 301s of 16,360 lb (7420 kg) st each

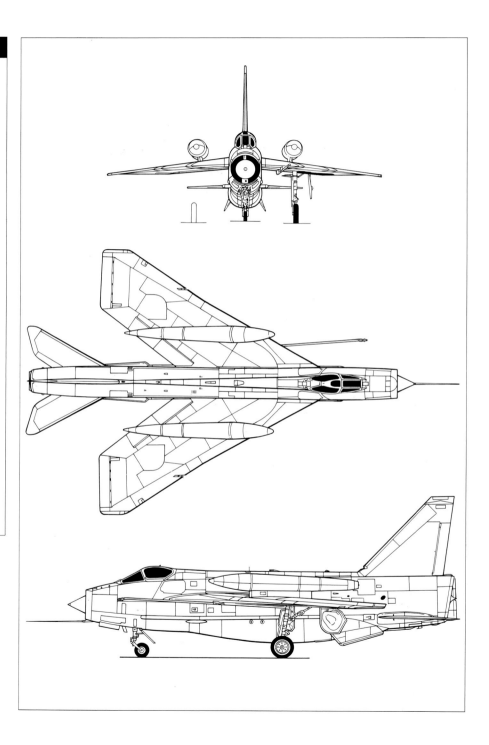

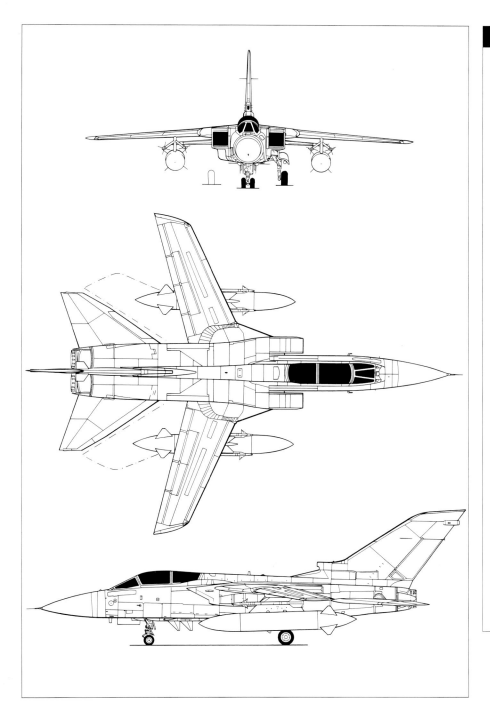

Flown from September 1988 to January 1993 with No 229 OCU and then Nos XI, 23 and 25(F) Sqns from Coningsby, in Lincolnshire, and Leeming,, in North Yorkshire

Type: tandem two-seat air defence interceptor

Powerplant: two (approx) 9000 lb st (4082 kgp) dry and 17,000 (7711 kgp) reheat Turbo-Union RB.199-34R Mk 104 turbofans

Performance: (estimated) max speed, 920 mph (1480 km/h) or Mach 1.2 at sea level, 1450 mph (2333 km/h) or Mach 2.2 at 40,000 ft (12,190 m); time to 30,000 ft (9145 m), 1.7 min; operational radius (combat air patrol with two 330 Imp gal/1500 l drop tanks and allowance for two hrs loiter), 350-450 mls (560-725 km); ferry range (with four 330 Imp gal/1400 l external tanks), 2650 mls (4265 km)

Weights: (estimated) empty equipped, 31,970 lb (14,500 kg); normal loaded (four SkyFlash and four AIM-9L AAMs), 50,700 lb (30,000 kg); max, 56,000 lb (25,400 kg)

Armament: one 27 mm IWKA-Mauser cannon plus four BAe SkyFlash and four AIM-9L Sidewinder AAMs

Status: first of three F.2 prototypes flown on 27 October 1979, and first of 18 production F.2s (including six F.2Ts) flown 5 March 1984. Deliveries of F.3s (against RAF requirement for 147) commenced in 1986

Notes: the Tornado F.3 is the definitive air defence version for the RAF of the multi-national (UK, Federal Germany and Italy) multi-role combat aircraft. It differs from the F.2 in having Mk 104 engines with 14-in (36-cm) reheat pipe extensions, automatic wing-sweep selection, a second inertial platform and provision for four rather than two AIM-9L Sidewinders

Dimensions: Span (25° sweep), 45 ft 7¼ in (13.90 m), (68° sweep), 28 ft 2½ in (8.59 m); length, 59 ft 3 in (18.06 m); height, 18 ft 8½ in (5.70 m); wing area, 322.9 sq ft (30.00 m²)

Dassault-Breguet Mirage 2000C*

Currently flown as part of a three-year 'exchange' posting with 2° Escadrille, as part of 5° Escadre de Chasse, at Orange in southern France

Type: single-seat (2000C) air superiority; (2000N) two-seat low-altitude attack fighter; or (2000B) conversion trainer
Powerplant: one 14,460 lb st (6500 kgp) dry and 21,385 lb st (9700 kgp) reheat SNECMA M53-P2 turbofan
Performance: max speed (short endurance dash), 1550 mph (2495 km/h) above 36,090 ft (11,000m), or Mach 2.35, (continuous), 1452 mph (2337 km/h), or Mach 2.2, (low-altitude without reheat and with eight 551-lb/250-kg bombs), 695 mph (1118 km/h), or Mach 0.012; max initial climb 56.000 ft/min (2845 m/sec); combat radius (intercept mission with two 374 Imp gal/1700 l drop tanks and four AAMs), 435 mls (700 km)
Weights: (2000C) empty, 16,534 lb (7500 kg); max take-off, 37,480 lbs (17,000 kg)
Armament: two 30 mm DEFA554 cannon and (air superiority) two Matra 550 Magic and two Matra Super 530D AAMs, or (close support) up to 13,890 lb (6300 kg) of ordnance on five fuselage and four wing stations
Status: first of seven prototypes flown 10 March 1978, with production tempo of six monthly
Dimensions: span, 29 ft 1 ½ in (9.13 m); length, 47 ft 1¼ in (14.36 m); height, 17 ft 0 ¾ in (5.20m); wing area, 441.3 sq ft (41,000 m²)

* This three-view drawing depicts the prototype Mirage 2000, rather than the definitive single-seater currently in service

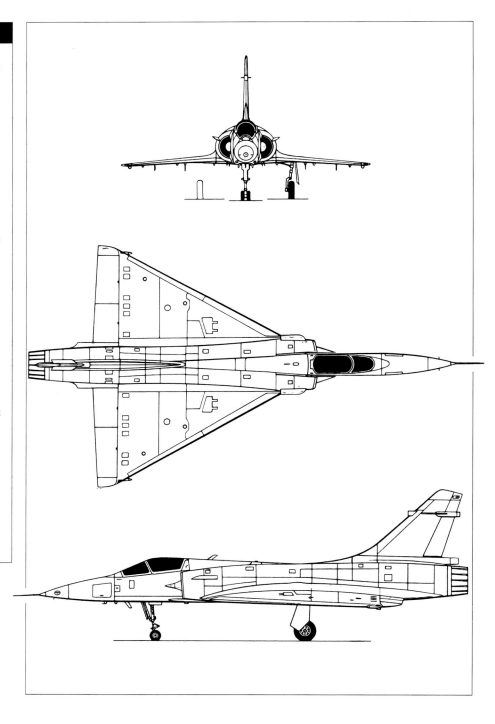